for
Help

the
No Blame Approach
to Bullying

by
George Robinson
Barbara Maines

Reprinted	February 1998
Revised	January 2000
Reprinted	March 2003, November 2003

Cover design and illustrations by Barbara Maines

Photographs: Pupils at Dr Bell's School, Bristol
Hannah's friends
Daniel, John, Joss and Melanie.

Lucky Duck Publishing
3 Thorndale Mews, Clifton, Bristol, BS8 2HX
Tel: 0117 973 2881
Fax: 0117 973 1707
e-mail   publishing@luckyduck.co.uk
website   www.luckyduck.co.uk

ISBN 1 873942 86 9

Contents

Foreword

George and Barbara thank:

- all the people who have made contributions to this book
- the many people who came to our courses with an open mind and went away eager to try the No Blame Approach
- those who came to the courses resistant, who expressed frustration and irritation, and who wrote or telephoned weeks later to tell us of their successes in using the method.

What's in a name?

We devised the No Blame Approach in 1991 in response to a specific request to help alleviate the suffering of a particular young person. The intervention was a response to a crisis and the name was adopted in haste. Whilst "No Blame" is an important ingredient, the procedure includes other essential elements:

- encouragement of empathy
- shared responsibility
- problem-solving.

None of these are made explicit in the name and, if we were to start again, we might choose another. It is too late now - we are stuck with it. If you come to this book with any reservations about the name we ask you to set them aside and read it with an open mind.

How did the No Blame Approach first start?

The No Blame Approach was first used in 1991 and it was described in our first book on bullying in the same year. (Maines, B. and Robinson, G. 1991b). This book starts and finishes with Andrew's Story.

Andrew's story. Part 1 - Spring 1991

The phone call from Andrew's parents requesting a meeting was not totally unexpected. I had been aware for a few months that he had an apt and rather uncomplimentary nickname and in class he seemed rather isolated.

I understood from the teacher who had accompanied a group of students on a field trip that the nickname had been used frequently on that trip and that several students had been spoken to about using the nickname and upsetting Andrew.

When the meeting took place with Andrew and his parents it was apparent that he and they were very distressed. He had been taunted with the name until two o'clock in the morning on the field course, cars drove into their cul-de-sac and students called out the nickname and Andrew had also been taunted when the family was showing a visitor from abroad a local place of interest. Andrew had wanted to return home early from the field course - only the support of another sympathetic student had kept him there - and he was considering abandoning his A level course.

I saw Andrew on his own having first asked him to write down exactly how he felt. He told me he felt upset, unhappy and pursued in every part of his life. He had tried to ignore the name-calling but it didn't go away, it simply became more persistent. He said he "felt like beating their heads in, like running away, quite unable to cope." I found out the names of the students who were the ring-leaders and saw them as a group. I explained to them exactly how Andrew was feeling and that he was considering leaving school. I told them that this was a real problem to us all and we must think about what we could do about it. At this point one boy spoke up and told the group that he had also been a victim of teasing during the previous year. There seemed to be a feeling of concern and I left the matter there, arranging to meet with each of the group individually a week later.

When I talked to them alone I discovered that they had all apologised to Andrew and that they were also going to intervene when other students used the nickname.

Head of Sixth Form.

When Andrew's teacher contacted us for help we advised her to follow the seven step procedure which we later named the No Blame Approach. We were very pleased that it worked so well and began to suggest it with increasing confidence as reports came back from teachers, parents and young people that the method was effective in stopping bullying. By the end of the year we were offering workshops and speaking at conferences, and early in 1992 the training video was published. In June 1992 a day conference was held at which teachers who had used the No Blame Approach met the press and completed questionnaires in order to assess the effectiveness of the method. The results were very positive. (See pages 72-73 for a discussion of the evaluation of the method.)

We expected this to be welcomed by those who are seen as experts on bullying, but we have often been surprised by the hostility and criticism that the No Blame Approach has aroused.

The criticisms seem to arise for two reasons:

1) a genuine misunderstanding and an expectation that because we propose a non-punitive approach we are letting the bully "get away with it," or even blaming the victim.

Eric Jones quoted in the Sunday Times (14/11/93) wrote:

> *"Parents want justice and action. If young people do wrong they must pay the price. We must not keep patting them on the back and saying 'nobody is to blame".*

2) a value position taken by some people, espoused by Kidscape, that bullying is carried out by "bad" people upon "weak" people and that a punitive and stigmatising re- sponse will solve the problem.

> *"Other children become chronic bullies because they:*
> * *Like the feeling of power*
> * *Are spoilt rotten and expect everyone to do what they say*
> * *Feel insecure, inadequate, humiliated*
> * *Don't fit in with other kids*
> * *Feel no sense of accomplishment."*
>
> **Stop Bullying. Kidscape.**

The advice given to the victims is:

> "*practice walking tall in a mirror. Bullies tend to pick on people they think are weak or timid.... You won't look like a victim if you walk as if you are seven feet high, even if you only feel two inches high inside.*" *(p. 5)*
> **You Can Beat Bullying - A Guide for Young People. Kidscape.**

There have also been calls for objective "proof", for rigorous research using control groups of children who are bullied, but to whom no help is offered. Other people have claimed that the method only works for certain types of bullying, and some have even suggested that it actually encourages bullying.

Michelle Elliott of Kidscape wrote in a letter to the Sunday Times (21/11/93):

> "*It seems to me that the No Blame Approach will only reinforce the attitude of joyriders, lager louts, muggers and others like them, who ultimately take no blame or responsibility for the consequences of their actions.*"

This criticism, though, completely misses the point. We are not saying that the No Blame Approach is the only method that ever works but we do think that experience has shown it to be usually the most effective and least risky for the victim. Neither are we claiming that every other method is somehow "wrong" (although we are very worried indeed by the harm that can result from punitive and stigmatising methods such as "bully courts", and the lack of first-hand accounts of their successful use).

What we are saying is, quite simply, that this is a method that is straightforward, easy to use and understand, and based on a sound and rigorous philosophy that fits well with principles that most schools will accept. Furthermore, it has been used with great success by hundreds of teachers, some of whom were initially very sceptical. Their accounts speak for themselves in a way that is direct and convincing. Read what they have to say, think about it, and decide for yourself.

We think that the method is successful because it recognises the importance and power of group processes and makes use of them, because it is straightforward and needs no obscure or mysterious expertise, and because it is a realistic approach for busy people to adopt. This is, of course, just the kind of subject that large-scale research might throw some light on, but that is not of central importance to us.

Many teachers who have been on our courses have asked us to write a comprehensive description of the No Blame Approach, and to answer some of the criticisms and misrepresentations that have been put forward. We have been slow to do this, because our time has been spent in training and developing new resources.

However, there is more at stake than sterile academic arguments. We know that our method works nearly every time that it is used, and has saved hundreds of young people from the pain and suffering of being bullied. We want it to be available to all young people in similar positions. We have, therefore, decided that it is time to offer a full account of the No Blame Approach, to assist and encourage those who are considering whether to use it, and to share with a wider audience the discussions and debate that have been going on among interested teachers who are in contact with us.

It is interesting to note that parents as well as educationalists support this approach. Smith and Sharp (1994) writing for the educational market say:

> "the No Blame Approach offers a useful practical method to add to the concerned adult's repertoire of techniques for combating bullying." (p. 205)

while Munro (1997) writing for parents states:

> "There is much evidence to show that a cycle of punishment and control is not a solution to bullying. Punishment tends to lead to more bullying because, after all, bullying itself is a form of punishment, control and domination.
>
> Some schools adopt a 'no blame approach' to bullying, that is taking a problem-solving approach, rather than a blameful and punitive one.....
>
> This does not mean being 'soft with bullies'. Victims are always given support and any bullying behaviour has to be stopped immediately. It means taking clear, firm and cohesive action.......... It is a long-term, and extremely effective, approach." (p. 96)

This book is a contribution to the process of discussion and analysis between practitioners. It is full of accounts written by real people working in schools in Europe, America, Australia and New Zealand. We believe that you will find what they have to say moving, compelling, sometimes passionate, but, above all, persuasive and convincing.

This book only deals with our work on responding to reported or observed incidents of bullying. A policy on bullying should also include actions to reduce the frequency of bullying incidents. Robinson, Sleigh and Maines, (1995); Maines and Robinson (1994b).

Chapter 1

Setting the Scene

Bullying in British Schools

The literature on bullying provides an interesting account of how the subject has developed and why the No Blame Approach was initially seen as controversial.

School bullying had a high profile in Scandinavian countries since the 1970's, with writers such as Pikas (1975) and Olweus (1978) providing valuable sources for later British publications. Though various articles had been written in the 70's and 80's, the first substantial book on bullying, by Besag, was published in 1989. There followed a variety of publications which all seemed to adopt a similar pattern: they gave a definition of bullying, identified the extent of the problem, usually included a section that searched for causes - often identifying specific characteristics of both bullies and victims - and generally concluded that schools could do much to reduce the incidence of bullying by using a variety of strategies to raise pupils' awareness of the damage that bullying could cause, or by creating safer environments and providing increased supervision.

What usually seemed to be omitted was any clear guidance on the strategies that could be used to deal with actual incidents of bullying. The one strategy that was promoted, especially by the popular press and T.V. programmes such as That's Life, was Kidscape's "Bully Courts". This type of intervention relied on searching for the truth, identifying the bullies and punishing them in public to show them that their behaviour was unacceptable.

In an article in the Sunday Times of 14th November 1993, Kidscape's approach is described as:

> "*putting classroom thugs before a 'bully court' of fellow pupils. Bullies could be 'sentenced' to apologise to their victims, be banned from the playground or even recommended to the headteacher for suspension.*"

Because the No Blame Approach was based on a very different philosophy, it was seen as somehow in favour of bullying, which led to public attacks on our work.

For all the media coverage, bully courts do not seem to have gained any popular support in schools. Smith and Sharp (1994) note:

> "*The school tribunal or "bully court", used as a means of dealing with bullying, presents something of an enigma.*

For a while in 1990/1991, it was perhaps the most highly publicised approach. Yet few schools appear to have used it, and it has proved difficult to get evidence about how well it works." (p. 205)

They go on to observe that, although Kidscape monitored eight schools using bully courts over a three-month period, and the number of students reporting they had been bullied was said to have dropped from 70% to 6%, no records were available. Smith and Sharp comment:

"This is a dramatic drop, but no further details are available in Elliott's article, nor are they now available from Kidscape, who apparently have not kept the records, or even the identities of these schools."

From 1990 to 1994 there was a very clear shift from punitive to non-punitive approaches. Smith and Sharp go on to suggest to teachers:

"focus on solving the problem ... encourage the pupils themselves to propose solutions to the problem ... the Pikas Method of Shared Concern and the No Blame Approach (but not the Pikas Direct Method, or bully courts) specifically avoid blaming or punishing." (p. 212)

This movement to a belief in non-punitive methods was due in part to the work carried out in Sheffield by Smith and Sharp, which culminated in the Department for Education (DfE) publication Don't Suffer in Silence (1994).

In 1991, DfE funded a major survey into the extent of bullying in schools and the effectiveness of various interventions. The findings and recommendations were made available to all schools. The DfE report included a study into the incidence of bullying from a survey of 6700 children, definitions of bullying, advice on the need for a whole-school policy, and suggestions on improving the school environment and on strategies to use when working with pupils involved in bullying.

The report mentions five methods:
1 The Method of Shared Concern
2 The No Blame Approach
3 Assertiveness Training

4 Peer Counselling
5 School Tribunals or 'bully courts" (on which the report
   added a caution that "the tribunal could provide a formalised route for bullying behaviour").

The first use of the No Blame Approach, in the spring term of
1991, coincided with the early planning by the Sheffield team,
and was, therefore, not included in the project. Peter Smith and
Sonia Sharp showed an interest in the method and referred to it
in subsequent publications (Smith and Sharp, 1994; Sharp and
Smith, 1994).

There is now an increased acceptance that non-punitive
methods are generally the most successful strategies to employ.
Rigby (1996) suggests that humanistic methods of dealing with
bullying will be more successful:

> "a No Blame method ... is more likely than other
> methods to result in the development of sustainable
> behaviour grounded in a process of internalisation rather
> than identification or compliance. To the degree that a
> student sees behaviour as being self-chosen, not in some
> way coerced or wooed into being, it is likely to be enduring
> ...
> Those who are really tough are sometimes actually
> encouraged by the threat of punishment. They see it as a
> challenge. We must also bear in mind that children are also
> influenced by the behaviour of dominant peers who used
> to bully others but have stopped of their own volition. If we
> can provide in a school more examples of these kinds of
> children, our job is made much easier. Humanistic methods
> offer better prospects of producing them."

(p. 221 - 222)

Chapter 2

Introducing the
No Blame
Approach

The No Blame Approach was not developed as a theory to be tested and tried - it was a response to a crisis for one teenage boy whose wellbeing was at risk. A teacher asked for help and we advised a simple, seven-step procedure. Our work on self-esteem, problem-solving and non-punitive interventions had been developing in schools for many years, but we had not applied it particularly to bullying. We wanted a strategy that was safe, that did not accuse, interrogate or alienate young people. We wanted a process that would improve relationships between young people and the adults working with them.

The intervention worked, and from then on we began to use this approach and to encourage colleagues to try it and to report back to us on the results. Early in 1992 the training film was published and a programme of inset was underway which, to date, has trained about 30,000 people, mainly teachers, psychologists and education welfare officers.   ·

From controversial beginnings, the No Blame Approach is now generally accepted as a safe and helpful intervention. A number of evaluation studies support this claim and research findings were presented in a paper to the British Association (Maines & Robinson, 1994a).

However, because the work grew gradually and evolved out of practise, it has so far been presented only in the format of training materials and papers. The present publication includes a more coherent review of the origins of the work, accounts of the use of the No Blame Approach and results of the evaluation studies.

Comparison with the Method of Shared Concern

In 1992 we enjoyed a meeting with Anatol Pikas, author of another non-punitive intervention, the Method of Common (or Shared) Concern (Pikas, 1975 and 1989). The two approaches have several features in common, but there are also some significant differences:

1 Pikas speaks first to the bullies in order to protect the victim from further damage in revenge for "telling". We have found it worthwhile to take this risk on behalf of the victim, in exchange for the powerful influence that the victim's story will have on the group.

2 Pikas speaks separately to each member of the bullying group. We suggest that the first meeting should be with all

those who are involved in the bullying, or know about it, even if they were colluding only by failing to intervene. The group can also include friends of the victim.

3 We share with Pikas his approach of identifying a "Common Concern" which leads on to problem-solving. However, we place more emphasis on heightening the concern by telling the bullies and the rest of the group how the victim feels.

4 Pikas aims to create a partnership between the bully and the therapist in a shared common concern. We work much more with group dynamics to change behaviour.

5 By the very nature of Pikas' interviews with the bullies, and his second step (of getting agreement from individuals that the bullying has happened), he is attaching a bully label. Our approach never publicly attaches any label - the bullies are just members of the group.

Richard Gilham uses both approaches (see p. 92).

In January 1994, we met Dan Olweus at a conference in Adelaide. Dan is one of the most acclaimed writers on the subject of school bullying. He advised us that a reliable evaluation of the No Blame Approach would require a control group of young people in distress, for whom no help would be offered. His point was that some victims report at the point of crisis from which there could be a spontaneous remission. This factor would distort the statistics and attribute a falsely high success rate to the reports. Whilst we acknowledge this possibility, we would not be prepared to research in this manner. The No Blame Approach is simple and seems to work nearly every time. When bullying is reported it would be inexcusable to take no action for the sake of scientific rigour. We are content to report on the effectiveness of the work through personal (but at the same time often very powerful and convincing) accounts from those involved. All we need to know is:

- Has the problem got better?
- Has it stayed better?
- Was it a comfortable and easy process?

The contributions in this publication will provide answers from practitioners who have used the No Blame Approach in a variety of circumstances. Some contributors were initially very sceptical. One found the training very frustrating and went away disgruntled and suspicious. He called us a few weeks later and said, "You just have to try it to see how well it works!" Some tried it because it "felt the right thing to do", and some because "at least I can tell the parents I am going to do something positive".

Teachers frequently say to us, "We like the idea but the parents won't agree. They want the bullies punished." That has not been our experience. We have presented many parent workshops and, although it is true that parents may be very distressed and initially ask for punishment, what they want above all else is for the bullying to stop. With few exceptions, we have found that parents are willing to try our approach. They know that punishing the bully might make things much worse. We include in this publication two accounts specifically written from the parental viewpoint, but in addition many of the contributors are parents who would choose this intervention for themselves or their own children.

Chapter 3

Bullying in schools and society

Most of the attention devoted to bullying has focused on its effects on school children when their peers bully them. There is now a growing interest in other forms of bullying - in the workplace, in pre-school or neighbourhood environments, or where adults bully children or pupils bully teachers. We are interested in all aspects of bullying, but most of our experience and knowledge relates to bullying in schools. Many of the principles can, of course, be applied to any other setting where similar behaviours and effects are found.

Walk past any school playground and take some time to watch the children playing. There will be plenty of noise and movement as they create their games and you will see many smiling faces. Watch carefully and look closely at the expressions on the faces of some of the children who seem to be left out, on the edge of things. You will see some who are suffering, who do not enjoy this free time, and maybe some who are being tormented by their peers. For these children their time at school, nursery, or college is a real misery and this is a misery that is with them all the time - not just when they are excluded or tormented. It is with them in class, on the way to school, and on Sunday evenings when the next school week approaches. It is with them when they are in bed at night and it is the first thing they think about when they wake up in the morning. This is what bullying really means. It is not to do with occasional or random acts of nastiness, because these can usually be avoided. Bullying causes those who experience it to suffer a continuing distress, which ranges from unease to absolute terror.

The popular children's literature that was read twenty and thirty years ago included many stories of school life. If these stories were taken to represent the real lives of children at the time, we would think that they all went away to boarding school at an early age, returning to their families for long idyllic summer holidays. Whilst away from home they suffered a passing bout of homesickness and then settled into the spirit of school life. For those who believe that bullying is just a facet of the present violent and competitive world, an examination of children's literature will quickly change their minds. You will read stories of physical violence and, at the boys' schools, even torture. In the stories for girls, there is a different sort of behaviour. It may be teasing or name-calling, or the process by which one person is excluded from the social group or just has a trick played upon her which causes humiliation. Just the same, it is torture. It hurts just as much.

In these stories, you will not be persuaded to take sides with the victim. The group represent the popular and healthy model of young people of their time. They were learning to stand up for themselves, to show courage and strength of character. A child who complained about the way her peers treated her would be told not to tell tales, and if she did, her popularity would slide even further. These unfortunate youngsters were portrayed as having some undesirable characteristics. To listen sympathetically to their accounts of suffering would have been viewed as encouraging their weakness and dependence. The best way out of their dilemma was to learn to stand on their own two feet.

For a few this is possible. Out of their desperation, some do develop strategies which improve their situation. Many are not so lucky and they continue to suffer for years. Some take avoiding action and withdraw from the company of other children or even from school altogether. A few withdraw from life. Most survive to remember the events. They can recount their stories with accuracy, recalling specific details, names, words and feelings. These memories may go back decades and will remain with the person for the rest of his or her life They are significant determiners of emotional and psychological development.

It is important to understand what is meant by bullying. It is also important to differentiate bullying from other unpleasant and antisocial behaviours. This is not because they are unimportant, but because a quite different response may be needed.

Most people have a clear idea about the way bullying works. They know that there is an element of intimidation or power used by the bully with the deliberate intention to hurt the victim. This may be physical harm but more often it is emotional or psychological harm, - behaviours such as teasing, exclusion, name-calling or the threat of physical aggression if the victim does not provide favours to the bully. A crucial and defining characteristic of bullying is that it goes on and on. The victim lives in constant fear of the next encounter, knowing that the behaviour will be repeated over and over again. The misery is with the victim most or all of the time.

Kids may sometimes get hurt or frightened by an encounter with another child who shouts, pushes, ridicules or even hits out at them. This may not be bullying if it is just an occasional incident. If you get in the way of a game going on in the playground, if you tell tales, if you spoil somebody's work, then maybe you will suffer some retaliation. It can be very unpleasant but it is not bullying if the situation can be avoided in the future. The child who is hurt is not in a continuing relationship with the aggressor. By taking some simple steps to avoid the repetition of the incident, the child will be safe from further harassment. Of course, this does not mean that teachers or parents should ignore random aggression. If someone is hurt then there is always a responsibility to confront the unacceptable response and teach different strategies. No-one has the right to hurt or frighten another person, whatever the provocation. This should be regarded as a principle of behaviour management, for which teachers and parents can be expected to have available a range of appropriate techniques other than anti-bullying interventions.

There is another sort of behaviour that is very harmful and damaging to the recipient but which may not be susceptible to anti-bullying strategies. It is based within a value system that is often shared by family members, friends or other powerful influencers. When an individual or group is subjected to abuse, harassment or loss of rights or dignity because of a difference in skin colour, culture, religion or nationality, it is referred to as racism. The persecution is often explained by the perpetrators in terms of some belief which they feel justifies the behaviour. Family or societal values may themselves support these ideas, reinforcing the position held by the child. Young people come into the school from a variety of backgrounds. They are presented with a code of morals and related behaviours. This is often referred to as the ethos of the school and may be included in a code of conduct with statements such as: 'respect the rights of others'. Parents have probably read the code in the school handbook and most will share the values promoted in school. Sometimes there may be differences, and these can cause confusion to a child who is expected to believe both teachers and parents. Occasionally these differences relate to fundamental attitudes about issues such as race, religion or gender roles. If a child hears racist language at home then it is hardly surprising that this spills over into school. We would expect a teacher to confront any pupil who uses a racial slur towards another child. The behaviour requires a response and the teacher will hope to influence the attitude of the child involved. This will then require the child to choose between parent and teacher and decide who is 'right' and who is 'wrong'.

Anti-bullying strategies are strong and influential techniques that have a significant impact on behaviour and attitudes. If they are employed to influence racist behaviours in a child whose values are supported by parental attitudes, then there will be a risk of damage to the child's respect for parent or teacher. Similar situations may arise when parental views on issues such as gender roles, the value of higher education, school uniform or swearing are different from the views expressed by the adults in school. In these cases, special techniques are needed to influence values without any threat to the relationship.

Educators have a right and a responsibility to influence values. This is the most difficult task they undertake and can only be achieved over time.

This publication, however, concentrates on dealing with bullying, not with clashes of values.

Chapter 4

The frequency of bullying in schools

How often does it happen?

There has been a lot of publicity about bullying during the last two years, with articles in newspapers and some heartbreaking stories of the fate of a number of teenagers. A popular television programme took up the cause and interviewed the families of two young people who took their own lives when bullying became too much to bear. Funds were made available for a bully helpline and the lines were jammed with calls from young people needing to talk about their situation. All of a sudden, the topic has become one of national interest and there is a belief that "bullying is on the increase". This may appear to be the case merely because the public interest in the subject has increased. It does not necessarily indicate that there is more bullying happening in our schools than there was twenty or fifty years ago.

A researcher trying to clarify this situation faces several problems. Firstly, there is little data available. Any information about bullying in the past must rely mainly on the recollections of adults who look back on their own days at school. Our memories can play tricks, and feelings may be intensified or reduced by the passage of time. Secondly, all of the evidence has been collected by asking children and young people about their experiences. This is generally done by questionnaire. We cannot be sure that this method will provide an entirely truthful picture. Even when confidentiality is promised, there may be a reluctance to admit to victimisation and an even greater likelihood that the aggressors would not give an accurate picture of their behaviour. It has been shown that, when the researchers take some time to describe bullying before administering the questionnaire, they get a higher response rate. If they ask 'Have you been bullied?' the percentage agreeing may be as low as 5%, but when they explain that it includes name-calling, teasing, threatening, taking property and exclusion from games and friendship groups, then the figure goes up considerably.

The most reliable figures come from an important study carried out at Sheffield University, funded by the DfE. The researchers surveyed 6700 young people in 24 schools (17 primary, 7 secondary) and found that 27% of primary pupils and 10% of secondary pupils reported that they had been bullied several times during a school term. There is a slight increase in the age group ten to thirteen, around the time most children move from primary to secondary school. This is a time when young people face a significant change in their school lives. We have all heard the typical rumours that circulate amongst primary-school children who fear that they will have their heads stuck down the lavatories or some other initiation ritual performed on them by the older pupils at the secondary school. Teachers and parents may offer reassurance, but the myths are strong and seem to represent some significant change from childhood into adolescence - a rite of passage. When reassurance is offered about one particular fear, another pops up to take its place. The child is moving from an environment in which she has become one of the older and more important pupils into a much bigger and unknown place. In the new school she will be amongst the youngest and weakest, unfamiliar with the social patterns and physical surroundings. At this time children are more likely to talk to parents and other adults and may easily express their worries as a fear of bullying. As the young people progress through their school life, they report less bullying. The frequency of the incidents perceived by the students as serious seems to remain the same but the less hurtful incidents are not reported, either because they reduce or, more likely, because they are seen to be part of everyday school life, hardly worth mentioning.

None of the surveys has found one single school where there is no bullying.

Chapter 5

The parents' stories

During in-service days we have presented to teachers we are often told:

> "*Though we can accept your approach to bullying the parents won't accept it - they want retribution.*"

In the sessions we run for parents the recurring theme we hear is:

> "*We want one thing... we want the bullying to stop.*"

The Anti-Bullying Campaign, a national parent organisation actively promotes the No Blame Approach.

The following two stories are typical of many similar situations that have caused intolerable pain and distress to countless children and those who care for them. The worst parts of this suffering could be avoided if parents and professionals could set aside deeply held, taken-for-granted beliefs about bullying and how best to deal with it.

This particular story is told from the dual perspective of a parent whose child was bullied, and who is also a teacher-trainer specialising in delivering school-based training on how to reduce bullying in schools, and how to deal with it effectively when it occurs.

Mary's Story

Between 1989 and 1992 I worked at the Faculty of Education at Bristol Polytechnic (now the University of the West of England). During this time I worked closely with George Robinson, and was particularly struck by the work he and Barbara Maines were developing on the subject of bullying.

After participating in one of their training days on the No Blame Approach, I introduced their work to one of the groups of teachers that I was working with and suggested that they should trial this approach in their schools. After a few weeks, I sought feedback on the No Blame Approach. All of the teachers who had tried it responded positively, saying that they had experienced real success and that they intended to carry on using it. I began to realise how effective this technique, and some of the associated ideas, were.

In 1992, as requests from schools for training increased, I began to deliver training as an associate of Lucky Duck Enter-

prises. I continue to work on this basis - travelling regularly to schools around the country and training staff. I suppose that I could now claim a degree of expertise in the subject.

My own professional engagement with the subject of bullying sets a backdrop to this story, which concerns my eldest daughter, who was bullied at her primary school in 1992. Perhaps the most distressing (and certainly the most frustrating) aspect of the story was the way that it followed the pattern which George and Barbara frequently describe, and which I have learnt to use in my own training sessions. A child gets bullied - this is brought to the attention of the school - the school applies a traditional response by trying to equip the victim with skills for dealing with bullies and also punishes the bully - the bullying gets worse and is accompanied by threats about what will happen if the school finds out - the victim tries to hide the bullying from parents and teachers, fearing that it will get worse.

Mary did not tell us that she was being bullied. She did not understand that she was being bullied, but she did know that someone was being constantly cruel to her and it was obvious to us that she was losing her former enthusiasm for school. It seemed as though she had already learned that it was not a good idea to report peers' misdemeanours to teachers, or even to parents (in case they inform teachers).

Our increasing concern about Mary's growing unhappiness led us into some gentle questioning and careful listening. After several 'sessions' she admitted that one of the boys in her class was picking on her, with occasional support from his friends. This apparently took the form of regular teasing, occasional threats of physical violence and very occasional pushing and hair-pulling. She begged us not to tell the school, clearly feeling that a barely tolerable situation could get worse if she was identified as a sneak. Reminding her of my status as a teacher and as a part-time teacher trainer with some knowledge of bullying, I persuaded her of the efficiency of telling the class teacher. How else could the teacher help? I promised her that this course of action would help, suggesting that the teacher would probably just watch her and her interactions a bit more closely for a while.

I telephoned the Headteacher, told her about Mary's experiences and stressed her anxiety about possible interventions. I asked her (the Head) to inform the class teacher and requested that the boy should not be singled out or punished at this stage. She agreed to my request.

The following afternoon Mary returned from school quite

distressed. Her teacher had drawn her aside in the morning for a quiet chat and had 'counselled' her to stand up for herself and fight back. (Many schools continue to advise the victims of bullying in this way - some even institute formal assertiveness training for victims as if in some way the bullying is their own fault, with the ultimate implication that it is they who must change). Mary, who I regard as genuinely assertive and a good judge of what is required of her in a given situation, had taken her teacher's advice. When abused and jostled in the playground, she pushed her antagonist and told him to leave her alone. She had then been wrestled to the ground amidst a crowd of jeering boys and was convinced that she would have been seriously hurt if a playgroup attendant had not broken things up. For the remainder of the school day, she had suffered a series of taunts and threats.

This time, when Mary pleaded with us not to tell the school about what had happened, we listened and agreed to do nothing (despite our knowledge of the subject and our overwhelming desire to do something to protect our child). Over the next few days Mary gave us various reports of ugly-sounding incidents, usually prefaced by 'this wasn't really bullying, but ...' Eventually I could not bear it any further and I pulled adult rank and told Mary that I was going to see the Head. I telephoned her and booked to see her before school the following morning.

I thought that the meeting went well. The Head listened to my report and showed genuine concern. She acknowledged that the school was aware that it had a problem in managing the behaviour of a group of boys in Mary's class and that Mary's antagonist was causing particular difficulties. I stressed that I did not want this boy to be punished, as I thought this would make Mary's life even more difficult. I also expressed dismay at the advice that she had previously been given, and the consequences of her having acted on it. The Head reserved the right to reflect on the problem before deciding on any particular course of action. I left the meeting feeling that at least Mary's suffering was coming to an end. That day Mary came home in tears. Apparently, the Head called the boy out in front of the whole school during morning assembly. She had told everyone that this boy was a bully. While giving him the occasional push, she had advised everyone that they should not play with him (girls in particular) and that they should make it clear to him that they would not tolerate bullying in their school. Mary was aware that all her classmates knew that she was the victim.

During the morning playtime the boy approached her, accusing her of grassing him up and kicked her on the leg (causing a large bruise). He cursed at her and told her that he was going to beat her up. A chase around the playground ensued, with Mary eventually heading into the school building and locking herself in a girls' toilet after an older girl grabbed the boy, thus allowing Mary the time to make her getaway. She had spent the rest of the day in a state of fear, convinced that sooner or later she was going to be beaten up.

I telephoned the Head and gave her Mary's account of the day's events. She expressed horror and particular concern that this had happened without her knowledge despite the warnings to the boy and her call for vigilance from staff. She informed me that she would be taking serious action against the boy, implying that he would be suspended if not excluded from the school. I could not find it in myself to describe my belief that she was culpable and that her actions had exacerbated the situation - I myself and many other teachers have followed the same, or similar procedures with perfectly good motives - but merely resolved to move Mary to a new school.

Jonathan Coles

This is just one account of bullying in school. Indeed, there could be several different versions of this particular story if the key participants were asked to give their own accounts of the events. It is told from a parent's perspective. Its validity lies in the fact that it shares common characteristics with many children's accounts of bullying. Mary got trapped between a peer's need to inflict suffering and the school's inability to deal effectively with this remarkably common phenomenon. This led her to distrust the school and to want to hide the problem and the pain that she was experiencing, rather than to risk making it worse. Many of the tragic accounts of children who commit suicide, or attempt to do so because they are being bullied in school, have similar features. These drastic actions follow schools' attempts to deal with bullying - they do not precede them. In plain terms, it seems that the most common forms of intervention actually make things worse for the victims of bullying. This was certainly true in Mary's case.

Many teachers describe how children who are accused of bullying are likely to respond in one of the following ways:

- They claim that what they were engaged in was merely a

bit of fun - it was not meant to hurt and the recipient should have taken it in this spirit.

- They claim that the child provoked them and therefore asked for it - they were simply dispensing a form of natural justice.

To punish a child who has been found guilty of bullying is, therefore, likely to bring about feelings of injustice and indignation. Herein lies the danger for the victims of bullying. They are likely to be blamed not only for having spilled the beans, but also for the punishment. Thus a cycle of blame is established. Children who are punished for bullying tend to seek revenge and the obvious target is the child who got them into trouble. This secondary bullying is often more severe and is frequently accompanied by threats regarding what will happen if the school finds out about it this time. This often represents the critical point for the victims of bullying. They are trapped - knowing that they must face the bullying and be active in keeping it secret. In severe cases, it is easy to see how suicide can seem a real alternative. Schools can unwittingly contribute to this dilemma if they respond to the desire for retribution in incidents of bullying, without looking beyond the common assumptions about the efficiency of using punishment to alter behaviour.

The No Blame Approach to bullying sets out to break this cycle of blame and retribution. It gives children who bully insights about the effects of their actions and an opportunity to change their behaviour on the basis of these insights. Of course, it does not stop all children from causing pain to their peers; some children have such a deep need to cause pain, or such a habit of doing so, that only intensive therapeutic approaches would significantly improve their behaviour. However, even in these circumstances, such children will find it harder to operate if others in the group cease their support or collusion, and if friends of the victim strengthen their own resolve to protect him. This can be extremely positive for the child who has been bullied and also for the group (and the school) as a whole. One of the most common and distressing experiences of children who are being bullied is isolation. Peers withdraw their support and friendship, fearing that to do otherwise would be to run the risk of being bullied themselves.

The second story is told by the parent of a secondary pupil.

Anna' Story

My daughter Anna had enjoyed her primary school very much, especially her last year there, and had worked well and had many friends. So we expected few problems when she transferred to secondary school. She and everyone else in her class were asked to write down the names of any friends they especially wanted to be with when they transferred, and she wrote down at least seven names. We were all impressed by the care shown by the secondary school in this matter.

However, Anna came home extremely disappointed from her induction day at the end of the summer term before she started. She was not in a class with any of the friends she had named, and was very upset. Despite this, she started well in the autumn term and seemed to make friends with some nice girls from other schools. She had a few problems with the homework, trying to do it all much too perfectly, but the acting head of year helped her to make a feasible plan to cut the tasks down to size.

Anna had been hoping to be in the same class as her very best friend, who had gone to a different primary school, and when she found they were in different classes, she made every effort to spend breaks and lunchtimes with her.

Things began to go very wrong at the end of the first year. The best friend had made other friends who, it turned out, did not like Anna very much and began to say nasty things behind her back. As a result of this, Anna felt excluded; her best friend preferred the new friends, and had no time for Anna any more. She tried to spend more time with friends in her own class, but felt left out. She was also teased and made fun of, sometimes for being good at her work, sometimes for reasons she did not understand at all. She started to spend lunchtimes in the library.

As parents we decided to give it a little time to settle down. However, after two or three weeks, it was clear that the problem was not going to go away, so we went to see her form tutor. Unfortunately, Anna's form tutor from the previous year had left, and she had a new one who was also new to the school. This teacher said that, unless it was an academic problem, nothing could be done. She said she might talk to other staff and let us know if they thought of anything else, but we heard nothing. We had the feeling that we were seen as parents who fussed unnecessarily.

From then on, things went from bad to worse. Anna spent every lunchtime in the library, until she was totally bored with reading. Food was not allowed in the library, which meant that she returned home extremely hungry and bad - tempered, having been unable to eat her packed lunch.

Anna seemed quite unable to talk to us, but we knew things were not right because she lost her temper at the least little thing. She came home from school most days in a foul mood, shouting and screaming, slamming doors and sometimes just swiping things off the table, kicking, lashing out, the sort of behaviour that we had experienced from her when she was much younger but did not think at all appropriate for someone of nearly 13.

We tried very hard to help her to talk, often spending a whole evening trying to get something out of her, but she seemed unable to do it. We thought of changing schools, but this would have meant a fee - paying school in the city. We even considered boarding school. But Anna did not want to move to another school, as she felt she would have to start again and life would be just as difficult, or even more so. We knew that there were other parents who had similar problems, both at Anna's school and a neighbouring one - one child had transferred to a fee-paying school, another to a boarding school.

Up until then, we had not had a television, preferring Anna to spend time on music, reading, sport and playing with other children. She didn't seem to have missed having a TV, but now she asked much more urgently for a TV "just for company". We felt that we had to give in to this, as she did seem to be so lonely and spent so much time at home. She spent hours watching television; on the occasions when she was watching a funny programme, it was a great relief to hear her laugh.

It got so bad that Anna would not go out, even with her former friends. If people did invite her, she found an excuse not to go. She felt she was not really welcomed by anyone. It seemed that she was going backwards, and spending far more time at home than she did when she was at junior school. While all her friends were beginning to go out on their own or in small groups, congregating in the local shopping centre on Saturday afternoons, Anna would insist I went with her and take the bus so that she was in no danger of meeting up with anyone at school. She seemed petrified of anyone from school actually seeing her, being convinced that they would laugh at her.

One day a good friend of the family happened to come to supper, and within minutes had winkled the whole story out of Anna. It seemed that she was being teased for being good at her work, and also good at music and other things. She felt excluded, always the "fifth out of four" or the "seventh out of six". It was a relief to get the whole story. As Anna seemed unable to talk to us, we swallowed our pride as parents and asked this friend to take Anna out for tea from time to time, whenever her busy schedule allowed. We felt in many ways that we must be inadequate parents if our own child could not talk to us, and also because we had a child who "could not cope with school". This was exacerbated by the fact that we were employed in one of the human relationship professions.

Every so often during the term, Anna would say things such as "I wish I was dead" or "If I was dead, it wouldn't matter; it might be easier, nobody would miss me." The only thing we felt we could do was to explain that we would miss her dreadfully.

One day, about a week before the Christmas holidays, Anna refused to go to school. She said, "I just can't take it any more." We said "Well, you may not be going to school, but we are." Like many children and young people who are bullied, Anna did not want us to contact the school or the staff, in case it made things worse, or she "looked stupid", but we were desperate. We felt it was pointless contacting Anna's form tutor again, as she had told us nothing could be done, so we rang the teacher who had helped Anna with the homework problem in her first year. When we got through to her, she said, "Well, you have come to the right place. I am in charge of the No Blame Approach to Bullying for the school." We couldn't believe it, there was a person and a policy all the time, and we had been suffering the whole term for nothing!

This teacher saw us the very next day, after school. Anna initially refused to come, but in the end grudgingly consented. She did not attend school that day, and we all went to the school at 4.00pm. Anna placed her chair far away from the rest of us, but the teacher drew her in gradually with great skill. She listened to Anna's story, and arranged to meet her again in the morning during school.

The next day Anna came home looking brighter than she had done the whole term. The teacher had met with her, and asked how she felt, and had then explained this to the group of girls who were teasing her. They hadn't realised how Anna was suffering, and said they would make more effort to include Anna in the group. Anna was greatly relieved, and so were we!

Then came the Christmas holidays, and they were happier ones for knowing that the bullying problems had been sorted out. As soon as school started again, the teacher checked up with Anna, asking how it was going with the group. She felt it was going okay.

All in all, it took Anna about a year to get back to normal. Every time something went wrong, she would retreat into "Nobody likes me, I've got no friends". But gradually things improved. She became a bit more sociable. She was invited to birthday parties. A year later, she has been going out with a group of four friends, sharing a room on an orchestra trip with one friend, staying overnight with another. She began to catch up with her other friends too, and spent more time socialising than on schoolwork. However, we did not mind this a bit, as it was such a relief to see her happy and sociable once more.

She also became much more reasonable and easy to live with. Her self-esteem seemed to grow by leaps and bounds. Whereas a year ago, she would respond to a compliment with a scowl and "You're being sarcastic!", now she will smile and say, "Thank you".

Marian Liebmann

Sceptics might suggest that such changes are short-lived. We would respond that no change for the better should be ignored. With this particular story, we can provide some further details. It occurred during 1992. In 1996 we were approached by Sugar (Britain's Number 1 Girls' Magazine) who wanted to do a feature on the No Blame Approach with some type of personal angle. We gave them some contact schools and the following extracts are taken from the article "I'm best friends with my bullies" (Sugar 19 May 1996, pp. 36-37). They found Anna and the bullies/friends and asked for their memories of the events four years ago and, of course, how things were now:

The Victim

Anna: *At my lowest point, I remember thinking, "No one would miss me if I died". I couldn't wait to run home from school and escape from the bullying atmosphere.*

The Bullies

Sara: *Anna always had an answer for everything and I felt like she'd take over the group if we gave her half a chance.*

Ros: *I remember seeing her sitting on her own at lunchtimes and I feel really bad now that I didn't do anything at the time.*

Rachel: *We'd notice that Anna was depressed but she seemed so confident in class that we didn't think it was anything to do with us.*

Telling someone

Anna: *I felt like there was no one in the world who could help me. Mrs. Sleigh told us all about the No Blame Approach to bullying. It seemed like the perfect solution to my problem, as my main fear was that telling someone would get the others into trouble.*

Putting an end to it

Anna: *Talking to Mrs. Sleigh felt like a huge weight had been lifted off my shoulders. I explained how I was feeling and wrote it all down. I was relieved that I didn't have to be present when she talked to the others because I thought it would have looked like I was there to gloat and go, "Ha ha, you're in trouble now!"*

The Bullies

Ros: *When she (the teacher) told us how Anna was feeling, we felt terrible - we had no idea she felt like that.*

Rachel: *I was annoyed with myself for not noticing what Anna was going through and I wanted to hug her and say sorry.*

Sara: *I felt guilty. I was also shocked because I'd never realised that what we were doing was a form of bullying.*

Friends Again

Anna: *Almost straight away things went back to normal ... I'm happy and I've got brilliant mates.*

Ros: *Things were quite awkward to begin with because we all felt a bit embarrassed.*

Rachel: *I obviously wish it had never happened, but the No Blame Approach helped sort the situation out without leaving any bad feelings between us. It's actually brought us closer together.*

Sara: *Some of us are off to different sixth-form colleges next year and it's quite scary to think we won't see each other every day now.*

The last word

Anna: *Try not to worry about telling because with the No Blame Approach, there's nothing to be scared of.*

Accounts like this demonstrate the victim's fear that telling and getting the bullies into trouble will make things worse, and the corresponding relief at not having to confront the bullies, or even to be present.

Such accounts also challenge those who think that bullies need to be punished to make them feel guilt and shame. In fact, blame often forces the bullies to justify their behaviour, and thus diminishes their empathic responses.

These are nice kids, like so many kids involved in bullying. We suspect that when they leave school they won't turn into lager louts, joyriders or muggers. Their stories show that many people do not realise the effects their behaviour has on others, and that when they are told, the changes can be dramatic.

I can remember sitting on top of this shed with Jane and Emma. We were hidden from the path by the trees and bushes. Katy walked by and we started to call her names, really nasty things about the way she looked and dressed. She was angry and yelled back at us, "Sticks and stones will break my bones but names will never hurt me!" .... so we started to throw sticks and stones at her.

Looking back on it I can hardly believe that I did that. I was always nice to Katy. Her mother had died and she lived alone with her father who was quite old and he used to get her really unfashionable clothes. I felt sorry for her and I spent a lot of time looking out for her when other kids were unkind. Even so, on that day when I was hidden away with my best friends, I joined in without even thinking about how Katy must have felt. We laughed at the time.

Now I cringe at what I did when I was ten.

Melanie Maines - Graduate of the Royal College of Music

Chapter 6

Victims

It starts as soon as children start to play in groups.

We saw a TV documentary film of a group of three-year-olds playing in an outdoor setting. At one corner of the play area was a sandpit with some pieces of wood lying about nearby. There were three bright yellow hard hats and two boys had put them on and began building with the wood and the sand. Two more boys approached, hoping to join in. One picked up a hat and placed it on his head. This seemed to define the boundaries of the group: three hats and three boys. The fourth little boy continued to approach the perimeter of the sandpit, still hoping to join in the game. Without any discussion, the two original players began an attack. One lifted a big plank of wood and hit out at the new boy whilst the other used both hands to fling clouds of sand into his face. At this point the camera-person could not contain his outrage and began to shout at the two 'attackers' who looked quite horrified at this intrusion.

And it goes on into adult life.

This is an edited account of a tape-recorded interview about workplace bullying. The teacher who told us the story left teaching for a while. She returned and was a headteacher at the time we met her. At the start the interviewer checked out whether the experience might be too painful and was assured that, after an interval of several years, it was safe. *"It was quite a long time ago now, I've survived it, dealt with it, you know, changed"*. Ten minutes into the interview, though, Joan was in tears.

Joan's Story

Over a period of four years, I was the Deputy Head and the bullying was coming from the headteacher to all the staff and all the children. I was trying to protect the staff and the children from the worst excesses of her behaviour and so it all fell on me.

Whatever I did I was always wrong. I never knew what my job was, so how could I do it, because I had no idea really what the expectations were? I was never allowed to act as Head if she wasn't there; a supply teacher was never employed, so I was locked into my classroom and never allowed to be in charge.

Her behaviour was always shouting, aggressive; sometimes she would come in and shout at me in front of children, parents and other members of staff.

In the classroom next to me was a teacher in her first year of teaching. She was a mature student, a nice person but not very confident in her ability so really she needed someone to go in and boost her confidence - but what did the Head do? I didn't know this until after I'd left the school, as the teacher didn't tell me at the time and I would have said something if I'd known - the Head would go into her classroom after she'd gone home and snoop around and then leave messages on her table so that in the morning when the teacher came in to start her day there would be a message. I remember that one of them she told me was, "Your voice is not good enough for the children" or words to that effect. So there was this poor teacher feeling nervous; that was a good start to the day as you can imagine, a real put-down. That is the way the Head behaved to everybody and she frequently lied. The final crunch point came because of that; she arranged to go away on a whole week's course but she expected me to run the school with no supply cover for a whole week, and as soon as she was out of school all the chaotic things that could happen did.

She had told me that she wasn't allowed any supply teacher cover by the LEA. It was paid for by the LEA at that time because it was before all the changes that have taken place so I phoned up the Authority to complain and discovered that she had lied and that they would have provided a whole week's supply cover if it was felt necessary.

I booked a supply teacher, then I contacted my union. Nobody helped me very much at all and I was in a really bad state then. I think that happened about Easter time and lasted through the summer term. You can imagine that the relationship had totally broken down.

The worst thing was that nobody did anything, no action was taken. We got to the end of the summer term and I had this hanging over me for the whole of the summer holidays and guess what, when I got back in September, my body wouldn't let me go on any more. I had swollen glands so I went off to the doctor, who thought I might have mumps. I said I'd already had it but he said I might have it again, so they did some tests and it wasn't mumps. I thought it was a medical problem but really it was symptoms in my body that were saying "Stop". Then I realised the effect was really awful, I had all sorts of symptoms, I couldn't put a coherent sentence together, my memory was dreadful. I'm not somebody who misses appointments but I would not go to the doctor's appointments - I walked about feeling faint, dizzy and sick; I'd never been like that before.

I felt very let down by the rest of the staff when the Union came in because they all had the opportunity of standing beside me and that Head would have gone if they'd done that but they didn't.

People aren't often prepared to stand up and be counted but it would have been in the best interests of the school. The only thing I wondered afterwards was whether I should have gone to the Governing Body. I'm sure they must have know something was going on but I didn't really know what to do. I suppose that's another thing, you don't know what to do for the best.

I shouldn't really have carried on for as long as I did. I think that sometimes it's quite effective to write it down. I did actually do that. I had a file full of stuff but the LEA never dealt with it. I told them, and I showed it to the Union, but the LEA knew I had that file and they never looked at it.

Afterwards, I've forgotten who it was I was talking to, I said the Union had been quite nice and that sort of thing, and the other person wanted to know what they actually did, which was nothing really. Perhaps they were quite supportive towards me but as far as action went nobody ever dealt with it. I had to deal with it myself really.

(Interviewer): Did it give the staff a sort of cohesiveness, did you all sort of have somebody to complain against? Did you not get strength from each other because it wasn't just you she was doing it to it was everybody, or did it work in another way?

I don't think it did work like that, I'm afraid; you would think it might but it didn't. I think that most of them just wanted to keep out of the way and hope that nothing happened to them.

(Interviewer): When you talk to kids you say "Well why didn't you support the victim?" and they say "I was frightened that it would make it worse for me". Do you think that there was an element of that in your situation?

Oh yes, definitely, they acted selfishly, absolutely.

(Interviewer): One of the things I think we do when we're threatened, challenged and provoked by people who frighten us is we put on a face where we don't really show how hurt we are. Did you do the same thing?

Yes, I bottled it all up. That's another thing, maybe I should have let it all out at her, I took all the knocks and I was very angry about being cheated but I bottled it up. It all had to come out afterwards. For a very long time I couldn't speak to anyone about it without bursting into tears.

(Interviewer): At the time it was happening did you begin to tell somebody, did you keep it secret from your friends how unhappy and miserable you were?

No, I had friends that I could talk to about it. I suppose nobody else knew how to deal with it either. I used to lie on the sofa and just listen to music for ages - Vivaldi. When you get really depressed you don't go out, you don't want to do anything.

I'm still angry that woman got away with it and I shouldn't have allowed it to happen to me or to anyone else. As I say, nobody would stand a chance of doing that to me again. I'd just say, "I'm not standing for it and that's it".

I have dealt with it now, put it out of my way, changed my life and it will never happen again. It shouldn't happen to other people, either.

Stories from all age groups, nine-year-olds to forty-nine year olds, include the same significant points:

- a feeling of helplessness in the victim
- collusion by colleagues and friends who don't intervene because they are afraid
- a brave façade put up by the victim to hide the pain
- failure by those with responsibility (staff, LEA, union, parents) to intervene effectively.

The next interview was recorded in the Californian sunshine overlooking the Pacific Ocean but Phil's memories of pain and distress darkened the day.

Phil's Story

I was ten or eleven. What I remember most clearly is being a relatively new kid in the community; we moved from Chicago, which is a big city, to Park Ridge, which was a suburb about 25 miles out and it was a real change of culture. People in the suburbs were very money-conscious; there was a code of dress, even in second and third grade, that was very clear and foreign to me and very unimportant to my father, who would dictate what we would wear and how we could present ourselves in the rest of the community. What I remember is a period of about a school year where I'd be walking home from school and these two guys would follow me home and push me around, take something away from me, a hat or I had a briefcase that was corny to them so they'd tease me about that and they were just very cruel.

One of the boys was in my class. He was my age and then there was his older brother who was maybe a year older and they'd trip me up, push me around and follow me most of the way home. They didn't live in my neighbourhood and they weren't part of my group of friends. I don't think anybody even knew that this was going on; I'm sure that I came home crying many days and that I mentioned something to my Mum, because she'd be the one who was around, but the most response I can pull up from memory would be her basically fobbing me off and saying, "Oh, don't worry about them, this will stop, you're not hurt and I've got other things to do."

(Interviewer): Did you ever just sort of look for strategies like going home different ways or getting out early?

Yeh, I tried to stall and tried different routes but I really have this creepy sense that they came out of nowhere from behind me somewhere and it was inevitable. Sometimes they might be in front of me and I'd run into them so I really had a sense that I had to always be on guard. I kind of hear my Mum saying "It's not that big a deal, let's not stir up the neighbours - we don't want to look like weirdos", sort of in keeping with this class- and social-consciousness. That basically told me that I just needed to suffer this whole thing through.

(Interviewer): If you had the resources available to you now when you were a third grade kid, what would you think might have been a better way for you or for the system to deal with this problem?

If the parents and the school were really different, and really invited kids to speak up, they would have those skills and re-sources and then I would want any child to be able to say "This is what's happening to me", to know who to go to, a teacher or to understand the support services in the community enough; they really weren't ever pointed out to me as a child, I mean like here's someone you can talk to who has time for these kinds of things. I would want any adult that was aware of something like that to bring those guys and me together and say "What the hell is this?" and not stop until there was a solution, a resolution to whatever the issue was. You're talking about this phenom-enon being something of a natural process as a way of defining a group. I guess it would be one way to help kids include them-selves quickly into a group, find a place and not just be left as an outsider. 'Cos the scare of the experience was to consistently see myself as an outsider and almost foster that as a stance to the world.

(Interviewer): So while this was going on, these two guys were making your life miserable on the way home for a year or so, did you never really feel as though you integrated into the class you were in? You were always walking home by yourself?

Definitely, I look at myself now and I think I'm a fairly antiso-cial person in a certain kind of way. I think I took the role that was offered me, or the one that I could find and nurtured into something I could respect.

(Interviewer): So you built an identity that was forced upon you and sort of said "Well, I'll make this my identity".

Right.

(Interviewer): Can you tell me, Phil, how many years you've gone back for this story?

I'm thirty-nine now and so we're talking about going back twenty-nine years; and I still know the kids' names, I can still pull up easy pictures of what happened.
I think that there is still this puzzle in my mind: "Why did they do that?"

Phil's story includes some points we have often heard from victims:
* wondering "Why is it happening to me?"

- constant fear that it will happen again
- feeling like an outsider
- a desperate need for effective help from an adult.
- the long-lasting effects into adult life of childhood experiences.

Well-meant advice to ignore the problem is not only impossible to follow, but often gives victims a sense of failure and isolation.

The next story illustrates a point which came up several times in workshops we presented in France and Portugal to audiences from many countries. We began with an activity that asked the participants to translate the word "bullying" into their own language. Most did not have a single word for the behaviour, but all agreed that it happens. When there is no name for the activity there seems to be less effort made to stop it.

Michelle's story includes many of Phil's points but it also reinforces two of the teaching points we make:
- bullying is a social process
- the victim has a desperate need to belong to the group.

Michelle's Story

You asked me to write about the remembered feelings of being bullied in childhood. There were occasions when I was afraid to be in certain places, but often I just felt unwanted and excluded. My attempts to just "fit in" usually ended in dismal failure and a renewed attack on my self-esteem. The longer this carried on the more I thought I deserved this kind of treatment, that I must really be stupid, clumsy, or ugly, and that I was unworthy of being in the company of these other people who seemed to have everything going for them.

Looking back, I realise that the problem was never identified, never recognised for what it was, since in France, where I was brought up, there is no name for this kind of childhood trauma. The nearest word to describe it is intimidation, which implies a defect in the character of the person being intimidated, namely timidity.

Since the age of twelve I have asked myself and other people why this was happening to me, how I could change things, how these things happened, what was wrong with me, how I could make myself better, more acceptable, the same as these people who made my life miserable. I did not have a name for this thing that was happening to me, I even thought that it was a figment of my imagination and that no-one else noticed anything at all.

I lived with the feeling that what was happening to me was wrong and that in my attempts to fit in I was colluding with my tormentors in their attempts to belittle, ridicule and trap me. I felt that I should not be helping them and resolved on numerous occasions to walk away and keep my own company if necessary. But once in the company of my peers, I could not ignore them, I could not walk away, I could not pretend that I did not care. I remember the desperate need I felt to belong to a group. But I was always the outsider.

Once you have been identified as an outsider, it makes you a kind of social leper, a form of life so low that no-one wants to associate with you. Why should they? Even I saw myself as flawed in some way, mentally weak, without guts, for surely if I had guts I would not let them do this to me?

Looking back, I was probably inviting them to hurt me because subconsciously I must have felt that it was better to have a role in a group, even if it was to be the scapegoat rather than have no role, no place at all.

These questions that I asked myself at the age of twelve stayed unanswered for thirty years and it was only during teacher-training that I began to discover the dynamics of group interaction and interpersonal relations. Little by little I began to understand what was going on, and little by little I was able to undo the psychological damage that I had suffered as a child.

These experiences have left a mark which will never go away. They have left me unsure of myself, always seeking approval, ultra-sensitive to atmosphere and mostly unable to express anger and disapproval. I see myself now as a loner, more comfortable in my own company than with other people, unable to allow myself to react to people and situations spontaneously in case I should once more find myself facing the double-edged sword of needing to be part of the group and hating myself for going to any length to be included.

I am acutely aware of the plight of children who find themselves in similar situations, and I am constantly making all the children that I have any influence over aware of the effect of unkind words and concerted action meant to exclude other people. I am extremely grateful that the No Blame Approach has at last given us a safe and damage-limiting strategy for dealing *with this harmful practice. It breaks the cycle of fear: fear of retaliation, fear of being alone with a problem, fear of being hurt, fear of punishment, fear of the future, fear of facing up to ourselves and the fear of being different.*

Michelle Findlay, teacher.

Some particular quotations from this account are powerful illustrations of bullying as a social process:

- *I just felt unwanted and excluded.*
- *My attempts to just "fit in" usually ended in dismal failure.*
- *How could I make myself better, more acceptable?*
- *I could not walk away!*
- *I remember the desperate need I felt to belong to a group.*
- *I was always the outsider.*
- *I must have felt that it was better to have a role ... even if it was to be the scapegoat, rather than to have no role, no place at all.*

The reader might expect to find, in a chapter entitled "Victims", a description of these individual people, and of how they are **different** from other people who are not victims.

A social group defines itself by including its members. It then recognises those who are not members as outsiders and excludes them. This process strengthens the identity of the group members as being "in" but might involve hurtful, damaging acts towards those who are "out", thus creating victims.

Victims lack power, victims are hurting, victims live in fear of the next encounter and victims want it to stop. Bullying is so common that almost everyone, maybe everyone, knows what it is like to be a victim.

Chapter 7

Bullies

An article by Jack Straw, published in the Daily Mirror (1/1/95), is reproduced below with his permission. In it he gives an account of his own involvement in school bullying - in a group of ordinary boys picking on one of their number, for no obvious reason, and making his life a misery.

Burdened by Memories of Bullying.
Member of Parliament Jack Straw reveals the shame of his school days.

Eight lads aged 11 and 12 in one dormitory - all living together morning, noon and night. It was always likely to happen. It does in zoos. It does in the wild. And, unless you are very careful, or very lucky, it does in schools too. I'm talking about bullying - that dreadfully cruel process by which a group instinctively picks on the weakest of its members and dumps on that individual all the anxieties and fears of the group.

It's 37 years ago that I was one of those lads in a boarding house at Brentwood School in Essex. We never thought of it as bullying at the time. And in the two years that it went on, no adult seriously remonstrated with us for our behaviour.

Indeed, it never occurred to me until eight or nine years ago, when I got involved in education policy, that our behaviour then could be classed as bullying. It was only when I started reading about the mounting problem of bullying in our schools that I realised that's what it was. But for those two years at school, seven of us made life a misery for the eighth - Paul, I'll call him.

It wasn't classic bullying. There was no single big lad beating up a smaller one. Indeed, very little of the bullying was physical at all. It was verbal, psychological, insidious and, in many ways, the worse for that.

Paul had been "chosen" as the odd one out. I've no idea how the rest of us made that choice. Certainly, it was never a conscious decision. But the rest of us - each of whom, I guess, also found the frugal atmosphere of a Fifties boarding school quite hard to bear - picked on Paul. He smelt - but didn't we all? With only one bath and one shirt a week, who wouldn't? He was stupid - though his academic results were the same as the rest of us. He didn't join in - we made sure of that. Above all, he was different. I cannot for the life of me remember why or how, except that we had to make him different. And we did.

And besides all this, he had to put up with the sense of isola-

tion - that he was, literally, not "one of us". For, as I now understand, we had defined our group by reference to him. In the end, Paul could stand it no longer. He stopped boarding and, as he did not live too far away, became a day boy. He survived, at least, and recently he wrote me a pleasant letter from America, where he now lives, about the good times we had at school together. Not a word about the bad ones - which says more about him than it does the rest of us. But I still feel a sense of shame about my part in all this - and how we might have tipped him over the edge.

Of course, bullying can be a worse problem at boarding school because there are so few chances of escape. And, in those days, there was remarkably little adult supervision of boarding houses. That was left to senior boys, who'd often been through the same situation themselves. But bullying in day school in the nineties is still a huge problem that causes misery to thousands of pupils - and can sometimes lead to very much worse. Crime Concern has recently estimated that over two-thirds of children are victims of bullying at some time in their lives. They also found out that young people often did not tell an adult when they were a victim of a personal attack of some sort - whether it was bullying, a physical attack or racial or sexual harassment ... Above all, we've got to recognise the scale of the problem and how and why it happens. That's why I hope the story of my school days may help. For, if we'd been told that what we were doing was bullying, effective action could have been taken and we'd all have been helped - not just Paul.

Jack Straw M.P.

Here is the voice of a "bully" who is a successful public figure, not the kind of deviant that some writers suggested bullies become. The article provides anecdotal evidence to support some of our arguments:

1 Bullying is a group process, not a unique relationship between the bully and victim.
   - *A group instinctively picks on the weakest*
   - *He was, literally, not one of us. We defined our group by reference to him.*

2 Victims are not different - the group decides on the difference.

- *Paul had been chosen as the odd one out*
- *Above all, he was different, I cannot for the life of me remember why or how, except that we had to make him different. And we did.*

3 Bullies often don't know the effect they have on victims, but if they are told then their behaviour can change.
- *We never thought of it as bullying.*
- *I still feel a sense of shame about my part in all of this.*
- *If we'd been told that what we were doing was bullying, effective action could have been taken and we'd all have been helped - not just Paul.*

4 Bullying is, unfortunately, normal behaviour.

Crime Concern has recently estimated that over two thirds of children are victims at some time in their lives.

Given these figures, and the fact that bullies can become victims, victims can become bullies and that bullying is a group process, it is clear that most young people are involved in some way in bullying. This does not mean that we should see it as acceptable behaviour. What this book does is to describe positive interventions that will not only stop bullying but will also educate those involved to the damage that bullying can cause and the part that they can play in both prevention and support.

In the next story a teacher looks back to the time when he was a pupil and joined in, or at least colluded, with awful behaviour, even though he didn't like it.

Michael's Story

Gillian was the leader of the 'gang', which consisted of about eight people, both male and female. All were in the top stream of a large comprehensive school on a south-east London estate. I don't know why Gillian was the leader. She was more precocious than the rest of us, and she had a sharp tongue that nobody wanted to feel.

Joan was a new girl. She had moved from New Cross, and had decided that our estate was soft. She was intelligent and attractive to many of the young males. Maybe Gillian saw her as a threat. Joan wanted to join the gang. Diane, who was one of the more verbal members, thought it would be OK.

Several of us nodded in agreement, but Gillian decided that Joan would have to earn her place in the group, so she was told to meet with us during the break. We met in the sheds, eight with the one. We formed a circle around Joan and Gillian suggested that if Joan was going to be in, she would have to prove that she was tough. We all egged her on. Then from her bag Gillian drew a bunch of three daffodils. To earn her place Joan was going to have to eat them!

This was just a laugh, I thought, but it's OK - she won't do it. Joan said she wouldn't. Then somebody said "Chicken!", and Gillian said "Are you in or out?" All of a sudden Gillian had Joan down on a chair, and was forcing a daffodil into her mouth.

I looked on in horror - who knew what the daffodil would do to Joan? Who knew what chemicals the plant contained? I knew it was wrong, but I didn't step in. I can't really remember now but I expect I laughed, though inside I knew that it was wrong and dangerous.

Why didn't I step in? I felt shame afterwards and always made a point of trying to be friendly and supportive to Joan in all our future dealings. There were three other boys beside me there, and yet none of us raised a finger. We just waited until Joan had eaten the flower, then we withdrew. All I know is that we never spoke about the incident.

Twenty years later I was reminiscing with Diane on the telephone. "Do you remember Joan?", I asked. "Oh, she was the one that Gillian made eat the daffodil." Obviously the event stuck with Diane as well. I know that now I would step in, I would have told Gillian she was wrong, but I didn't and I still carry the shame with me.

This account, written 25 years after the event, like Straw's, supports another of our key assumptions: The power of the group forces many young people to condone bullying even though they do not like what is happening. Changing the group dynamics can empower young people to behave in the way they know is right.

- *I knew it was wrong but I didn't step in.*
- *I can't really remember now, but I expect I laughed, though inside I knew it was wrong and dangerous.*
- *I felt shame afterwards.*

- *I know that now I would step in.*

In summary, we think the stories in this chapter illustrate the point that we made earlier about victims - the important insights about them all refer to their social behaviour, and the descriptions of this behaviour would apply to most or all of us at some time.

For those very few individuals whose behaviour is persistently harmful to others, regardless of peer approval, and who seem unable to experience and respond to empathic understanding of victim plight, we suggest that another term be used to differentiate them from "normal" bullies. The vast majority of people involved in bullying are not disturbed or deviant individuals in need of intensive treatment programmes. Our work deals with this vast majority.

Chapter 8

What is the No Blame Approach?

What is bullying?

Not every act of aggression or nastiness is bullying and it is important to define the particular behaviours and processes before planning helpful interventions.

Bullying:

- is a social behaviour, often involving groups
- takes place repeatedly, over time
- involves an imbalance of power
- meets the needs of those holding the power
- causes harm to those who are powerless to stop it
- can take many forms: verbal, physical, psychological.

Occasional acts of aggression would not be described as bullying unless there was a continuing fear or torment for the victims. It is also important to differentiate bullying from "war-like" behaviours where opposing groups confront each other because they have different belief systems or territorial claims. These values may be strongly held through generations and are very resistant to change.

We do not differentiate between the "bullying - by an individual" and "mobbing - by a group" discussed by Anatol Pikas (1989). This is because we are describing situations in which, even if the bully is operating solo, her behaviour is usually witnessed in some way by others. If the witness supports the bully, however passive that support might be, then the behaviour is in some way owned by the whole group and the strengths of the group can be drawn on in order to confront the behaviour. Where the bullying occurs in complete secrecy, unknown to any witness other than the victim, then there will be no opportunities for intervention unless the victim reports the behaviour.

We have been to several workshops and heard accounts of incidents that have served to confirm our worry about the scale and seriousness of bullying at a group and institutional level. This book sets a challenge to its readers. We believe that effective interventions, which really combat bullying in schools, demand much more from us than just trying to convey to bullies that their behaviour is unacceptable.

Defining the terms

Our definitions are:

Bully - a person or group behaving in a way which meets needs for excitement, status or material gain and which does not recognise or meet the needs and rights of the others who are harmed by the behaviour.

Victim - a person or group that is harmed by the behaviour of others and who does not have the resources, status, skill or ability to counteract or stop the harmful behaviour.

The bully and victim are in a 'relationship' which persists over time and is characterised by the continuing fear that the victim feels, even when the bully is not there. In this way bullying differs from chance or random acts of aggression.

Bullying is "normal"

Many of those reading this book will have had some close relationship with a very young baby at some time in their lives and they will remember the self-centred and relentlessly demanding behaviour exhibited by that tiny, dependent human being. If babies were big and parents small then parents would undoubtedly be bullied! You may also remember, if you are a parent or have had close relationships with young children, the first time that a particular child was upset or cried because of sadness or hurt felt on behalf of another person or creature (rather than because some need or demand of their own was unmet). This emergence of "empathy" is a complex step in social and emotional development and is the basis for kind and unselfish behaviour.

We believe that it is not helpful to regard bullying as abnormal or evil. Many of us will remember standing back and at least colluding with, if not participating in, some hurtful behaviour towards another person because it increased our own sense of belonging, or made us feel relieved that we were not the one being rejected. Parents and teachers will often observe very nice kids behaving in a very nasty way when the need to belong to a group of peers is an over-riding factor. Today's young people in affluent countries are subjected to strong pressures by the manufacturers of trendy clothes and toys. Wearing the right trainers is all-important but they are only the right trainers if someone else isn't wearing them!

A willingness to step outside the peer group, and stand alongside someone who is rejected and harmed, takes strength and courage. It puts the "rescuer" at risk of rejection herself and the success of her stand is likely to depend upon her social or physical status. We are likely to take this risk only when we identify strongly with the distress of the victim and when we feel that our intervention is likely to bring about some change - when we feel involved and powerful.

Witnesses of bullying, or those who care for the victims, might have very strong feelings of anger and feel a need to punish the perpetrators. If an adult who is in a position of power uses her authority to stop the bullying then it may have a short-term effect upon that particular situation, but it is unlikely to change the status or identity of the bully and victim. There may well be a risk of further harm to the victim because the bully was thwarted ... "I will get you later!"

We suggest, therefore, that the primary focus of any plan to reduce bullying must be to change the behaviour of the bully and those who collude or stand by and do nothing. By involving the peer group it is possible to enhance the empathic responses of healthy members of the group. This in turn has an effect on the behaviour of the bully, who no longer has the group's consent to behave in a bullying manner.

Whole-School Approaches

Bullying in British schools is now recognised as a serious problem, and there is evidence from work reported in Sheffield and other areas that more and more schools are developing and implementing whole-school policies.

However, most teachers have not had an opportunity to attend a training programme and not all schools would choose bullying as a priority amongst all the curriculum pressures put upon them.

Most school policies state that:
- bullying is taken seriously
- bullying will not be tolerated
- victims and parents are encouraged to report bullying.

Some parents take this advice and seek an opportunity to report bullying but are often told:
- there is no evidence for the bullying
- the victim is at fault
- the matter has been dealt with by a "talking-to" or some sanction such as detention.

The change to non-punitive methods is not, in our experience, happening without the impact of persuasive, attitude-changing forces within the school. During our in-service training days most teachers are easily convinced by the logic and ethics of the No Blame Approach and cannot wait to try it. Some teachers are reluctant to put aside traditional and apparently common sense methods in favour of what appears to be a radical and different process. They also worry about the impact of non-punitive interventions on the "discipline policy". From these teachers all we ask is that they give the No Blame Approach a try; this will allow them to discover for themselves that it is safe and positive.

At the same time, some schools still have structures which might promote bullying. Teams and houses create the identity of groups. The members will belong only because others do not, and they will support the identity of the group by strengthening the boundary around it. Are we expecting too much when we ask a young person to discriminate between winning on the sports field through superior strength and using the same strategy to win power or possession in the playground? The very language of success - "I beat her, thrashed her, wiped the floor with her" - is applauded if it refers to a "game" and punished if it refers to a "fight".

The challenge to common practice

Many of the strategies in common use do not have a long-term effect on the behaviour of bullies. Inevitably, we approach bullying with strong feelings of anger and frustration towards bullies and sympathy for their victims. We have a responsibility to the students and their parents to respond effectively and the success of our intervention has to be measured by the degree to which it stops the bullying. Some of the responses often made by teachers are not successful in achieving this and we discuss them below. Please try to set aside any feelings of retribution towards the bully, and concentrate on the aim of changing the bully's behaviour, thus achieving the best outcome for the victim.

The "serious" trap

In training sessions we use two short video excerpts for discussion. In one a teenage girl is teased by her friends and tormented about her clothing. During the painful episode, she tries to belong by joining in the laughter against her and protesting that she will be at the party. In the second excerpt, a teenage girl walking with a boy is pushed aside by a group of three girls, forced to her knees and asked to drink from a can of drink which has been spat into. At this point, her friend goes for help and the group scatter.

The second incident is more violent and disgusting. When discussing suitable interventions, participants often choose to do nothing about the first incident, suggesting that it is best to monitor the situation and that almost any course of action might make things worse. However, after watching the second scene there is always a strong and often punitive response. Participants suggest:

- full investigation
- parental involvement
- comfort for the victim
- punishment of the bullies.

At the beginning of the training, we make a very strong teaching point which we believe is vital to the establishment of safety in schools:

> "*The seriousness of bullying can only be measured by the effects that are experienced by the victim.*" (Besag, 1989).

Although people often agree readily with this point, in the training session the second incident is nearly always taken as much the more serious, even though the girl in question has a friend who helps her. When we point out to the participants that the girl in the first scenario is probably much more at risk we often find great resistance. It seems that it is very hard for observing adults to make judgements based on a victim's suffering and to set aside their own response to the behaviour. A pupil is often suspended for fighting, even when the confrontation is playful, the protagonists evenly matched and nobody comes to any harm. No action can be taken against a pupil who gives a "look", even when it is a sign of repeated and violent aggression.

Similarly, the DfE document Bullying - Don't suffer in silence (1994) offers confusing and unhelpful advice by stating:

> *Dealing with minor incidents: Mild sanctions can be useful in responding to one-off incidents of bullying which*

do not result in actual physical harm. (p. 18)
    Dealing with serious incidents: For bullying which results in damage to property or person, a serious response should be considered. (p. 19)

Firstly, bullying is not an appropriate label for one-off acts of aggression.

Secondly, there is no evidence that physical assault is more serious than verbal or psychological bullying. It is probable that the reverse is often true. A broken arm, a bloody nose or torn clothing is very visible and the recipient is likely to be treated with kindness and pity. Name-calling and teasing are often dismissed by adults as not serious but these behaviours, especially common among girls, can cause great suffering and lead to tragic consequences.

A new approach to teacher intervention is required, in which adults always respond to the distress of a victim, regardless of their own views about how the pain was caused and whether it is justified.

Dangers of labelling

Although we use the terms "bully" and "victim" in this and other publications and training, we do not think it is helpful to use them as labels in school. We know that to call a young person by a negative name can affect her self-image, and must be difficult to accept for the parents, with whom we want to work co-operatively. We have even seen a video in which a teacher explains the system in use at her school, where bullies are required to wear a badge saying, "I am a bully!" Is such a label likely to decrease or increase the bullying behaviour?

Getting to the bottom of it.

It seems like common sense to question students about facts and reasons when bad behaviour is brought to our attention. When we talk to the young people, they often report that they give teachers the answers they want - the answers that will let them out of the room as soon as possible.

When you question young people about the facts, they will give their own perspectives. These are often contradictory, especially when a bully is trying to extract herself from blame. You may then be distracted from effective action in your quest for the truth.

Since 1991, we have been encouraging teachers to set aside

the need to gather information as though this were in itself an effective intervention. Imagine a typical scenario in which teachers separate the "witnesses" and either ask them to write down their accounts or subject them to a sequence of probing questions. Often the teachers' plan is to start with the young people considered to be "reliable" or "innocent" so that by the time the "main culprit" is questioned a good case has been built against her. If bullying is not a one-off incident but a sequence of behaviour over time, then how many events can be investigated in this way? How much time will be wasted before something is done to make things better? How much hostility and resentment will be provoked towards the victim during the investigations? The process is negative, unreliable and unlikely to pave the way for positive teaching of better behaviour.

This has been amongst the most controversial of our teaching points and has often provoked hostility from course participants where schools have used investigation as a cornerstone of the anti-bullying policy. It is only very recently that other writers have begun to recognise this issue, so it is gratifying to read, in "Bullying in Schools and what to do about it" (Rigby 1996), that our approach is supported:

> "Sooner or later, as the evidence accumulates and is sifted, there is a temptation to really "get down to the bottom of it" - to discover the truth, the whole truth and nothing but the truth. This can set into motion an increasingly complex process of examinations, cross-examinations, heavy documentation, etc. The temptation is strong, and for some teachers, irresistible ... We should ask ourselves whether we are going to spend precious time in tracing the origins of peer conflict and precisely and judiciously attributing blame, or alternatively using the time to resolve the problem and bring about a lasting reconciliation between two or more students. What we need to know, basically, is whether a person has been victimised and who may be responsible." (p. 191)

Even less helpful is to ask students to explain why they behave in a certain way. It is very hard to explain our actions, and perhaps impossible to do so in a way which will satisfy a teacher. We were recently told about a small pupil who undid the safety bolts on a climbing frame. His teacher asked him why he had done it, and his predictable reply was, "Don't know, Miss". The teacher became frustrated and we asked her why she thought he had done it. "Because he is disturbed and attention-seeking," she replied. Was the teacher really expecting the boy to reply, "Well, Miss, it is because I am disturbed ..."?

An alternative to the "Don't know..." is a justification for the behaviour. After all, this seems to be what the teacher wants ... "He took my pencil!" "She wouldn't play with me." "He said my mother was dead." We are unlikely to get an insightful and useful reply... "I have very little tolerance of this person and I show off to my peers by abusing her. This makes me feel popular and powerful and I learned this because in my last school it happened to me".

Does the question "Why did you do it?" call for a reason, an explanation or an excuse?

Changing the victim

Over and over again, we hear from victims that they have been advised or urged by parents, teachers or a group to change their behaviour in some way. They try to "stand up for themselves", "hit back", "walk away", "pretend they don't care", and each time their failure to act in a way which ends their misery just makes it worse.

Margaret Attwood's novel, Cat's Eye, illustrates this very vividly in its account of the relationships amongst the members of a group of teenage girls.

> *"You have to learn how to stand up for yourself," says my mother. "Don't let them push you around. Don't be spineless. You have to have more backbone."*
> *I think of sardines and their backbones. You can eat their backbones. The bones crumble between your teeth in one touch and they fall apart. This must be what my own backbone is like - hardly there at all. What is happening to me is my own fault, for not having more backbone.*
> **Attwood (1990)**

They feel it is their own fault that this is happening to them. It is not. Whatever their own inadequacy or difficulty, it is not their fault and it is not their responsibility to stop it. It is our responsibility and we must give them that message loud and clear if we are not to compound their unhappiness.

There is nothing wrong with assertiveness training for everyone. Social skills programmes can help many students who are having difficulties in making relationships. However, these interventions should not be linked directly with the victim's plight but with more general developmental work.

Punishment

Perhaps the biggest challenge for us is to advise teachers to abandon punishment as a response to bullying. This can be addressed from two points of view: pragmatic and ethical.

If punishment systems worked in society then unwanted behaviour would simply be stopped in the miscreants, and others would be deterred by example. Unfortunately, it is not as simple as that. The aversive learning process does not seem to work well for impulsive people with an "external locus of control", and no amount of anticipated punishment seems to deter them at the point of immediate satisfaction. This point comes across very forcibly in our work with young people in special schools for children with behaviour difficulties - if punishment had worked, they would still be in their mainstream schools. Our starting point, long before we began working on bullying, was to find alternatives to punishment for these young people. The criminal justice system provides evidence that, in many cases, the less punitive the sentence, the more likely it is that some rehabilitation can take place.

Social behaviours are learned, and the learning process is nurtured by encouragement, good teaching and experiences of success. There is no evidence that punishing a bully ever turned that person into a kind and helpful friend.

Punishment of a bully does not make life safer for the victim; in fact it will often make things worse when the bully takes revenge.

If you want to encourage disclosure and to work positively with bullies, then everyone in a school must know that effective action will be taken, but that it will not lead to punishment. We cannot agree with the view put forward by Eric Jones in Bullying - a practical guide to coping for schools (1991):

> Punish bullies. Record punishment and the reasons for it. Show him what you are putting on file and make him pay for whatever time it cost you to sort it out. (p. 23)

Bullying is an antisocial behaviour resorted to by young people when their social skills are inadequate or inappropriate, and we must respond in a way that will help them to learn better behaviour. Increasing their anxiety and alienation from us is not likely to do this.

The emergence of desirable social behaviours can start quite early, when toddlers are encouraged to understand their own feelings and the feelings of others. For example, sharing is a behaviour expected in families, pre-school and early school environments. But sharing is not a natural strategy. It is natural to eat all the sweets oneself. In order to gain satisfaction from sharing the child has to:

- understand and empathise with the feelings of a child who has no sweets
- experience praise from adults who reward the sharing with something more valuable than sweets: love
- establish a self-image as a child who shares and thus adopts this behaviour into her repertoire.

The important elements of social behaviours to be learnt are:

- empathy - the ability to "feel for another"
- altruism - the sense of self as doing good
- reintegrative shame - the sense of shame experienced when the behaviour causes pain to those who love the perpetrator, (very different from stigmatising shame where the perpetrator learns that she is a bad or rejected person).

Some traditional justice systems achieve great success using these influences - for example, the Navajo Peace Courts and Maori Family Conferencing. For an inspirational account of the introduction of the latter into the South Australian criminal justice system, see Braithwaite (1989).

The United Nations Convention on the Rights of the Child (1989) gives schools the responsibility to ensure that:

> *In all actions concerning children ... the best interests of the child shall be a primary consideration. (Article 3)*

It is hard to justify punishment as anything other than a traditional expedient. It is not in the best interests of either the bully or the victim.

The use of power

Bullying seems to be a clash between the powerful and the

powerless, but power is an acceptable feature of many aspects of human behaviour. Bullying can be viewed as part of a normal process of socialisation in which the group establishes its identity, which is reinforced by the exclusion of others. The strength of the group lies in its sense of cohesion; without somebody being out-grouped - that is, visibly outside the group - the boundaries are hard to define.

The use of power can be seen in the way the bully dominates, but the possible reasons for this - genetic, family background, low self-esteem, poor social skills, gender differences - are not discussed here. Whatever the reason, we take the view that we have bullies and victims in school, and that this is not a healthy situation. We need to provide a safe environment for all, and we need to question our solutions to the problem. The use of power to stop the bully may confirm to the bully how power can be used to intimidate the weak, and to suggest to victims that they need to be more powerful may leave them feeling even more powerless. The crucial element that we feel is overlooked in much of the research is the potentially pro-active role of those who observe and collude.

Colluders and Observers

Most intervention for bullies and victims concentrates on the relationship between them and pays little attention to the part played by the peer group. Even when the bully and victim have a one-to-one relationship, we have found that the peers know what is happening and are, therefore, colluding. A failure to intervene gives consent for the behaviour to continue. Often "innocent" friends will join in to establish their credibility with the leader, to be safe, to have fun. The victim, who might be in great distress, often tries to hide the pain, fearing that a display of misery will be seen as weakness and provoke even more extreme attacks. Thus the process continues. There is a need to make these pupils aware of the important role of a witness and to allow them to devise and practice safe interventions that they might make.

Two key elements in a policy.

Besag (1989) writes, *"The whole school system should be organised to support all children and staff so that no one child or teacher is left alone to try to resolve a bullying problem."*

Two distinct approaches need to be integrated in order to ensure that bullying is reduced:

- creating a school environment where bullying is seen by all to be inappropriate (prevention)
- helping victims and bullies (reaction).

The reader of books and articles on bullying will find a host of strategies and interventions planned to enhance the environment, develop the social and friendship setting of the school and supervise young people at play. These strategies will reduce the frequency of bullying, but, as young people feel safer, they may report bullying incidents more frequently, hoping for effective interventions.

Our Approach to Bullying Behaviour in School

If we take the view that bullying is an interaction which establishes group identity, dominance and status at the expense of another, then it is only by the development of "higher values" such as empathy, consideration, and unselfishness that the bully is likely to relinquish her behaviour and function differently in a social setting. If the preventive policy depends upon policing the environment, forbidding the behaviour, supporting and sympathising with the victims and punishing the perpetrators, then no lasting change can be expected.

The No Blame Approach

When bullying has been observed or reported then the No Blame Approach offers a simple seven-step procedure which can be used by a teacher or other facilitator. Note that each step has been carefully planned as a single part of the whole and variations may undermine the success of the method.

Step one - talk with the victim.

When the facilitator finds out that bullying has happened, she starts by talking to the victim. During this conversation the listener encourages the victim to describe how he feels with reflective comments such as, "That must be very hard for you ... So you have felt really upset".

The purpose is not to discover factual evidence about this or other events; if the victim wants to include evidence in the account this is always reframed to establish the resulting distress. For example a comment like, "They have all been ignoring me, nobody will talk to me." might be replied to with a response like, "So you felt really lonely and you were upset that you had nobody to talk to".

It is important that the victim understands and gives consent to the process. Sometimes there may be a fear that it could lead to further victimisation but when the non-punitive aspect is fully explained the victim usually feels safe, and relieved that something is being done. He may want the perpetrators to understand how much distress has been caused. Talking to someone else who has been through the experience might give further reassurance.

The facilitator should end the meeting by:
- checking that nothing confidential has been discussed which should not be disclosed to the group
- asking the victim to suggest the names of those involved, some colluders or observers and some friends who will make up the group
- inviting the victim to produce a piece of writing or a picture which will illustrate his unhappiness
- offering the victim an opportunity to talk again at any time during the procedure if things are not going well.

The victim is not invited to join the group to present his own account as it is possible that he will make accusations, provoke denial or justification and undermine the problem-solving approach.

Step two - convene a meeting with the people involved.
The facilitator arranges to meet with the group of pupils who have been involved and suggested by the victim. A group of six to eight young people works well.

This is an opportunity for the facilitator to use her judgement to balance the group so that helpful and reliable young people are included alongside those whose behaviour has been causing distress. The aim is to use the strengths of group members to bring about the best outcome.

Step three - explain the problem.
The facilitator starts by telling the group that she has a problem - she is worried about "John" who is having a very hard time at the moment. She recounts the story of the victim's unhappiness and uses the piece of writing or a drawing to emphasise his distress. At no time does she discuss the details of the incidents or allocate blame to the group.

Step four - share responsibility.

When the account is finished, the listeners may look downcast or uncomfortable and be uncertain about the reason for the meeting. Some may be anxious about possible punishment. The facilitator makes a change in the mood here by stating explicitly that:

- no-one is in trouble or going to be punished
- there is a joint responsibility to help John to be happy and safe
- the group has been convened to help solve the problem.

Step five - ask the group members for their ideas.

Group members are usually genuinely moved by the account of John's distress and relieved that they are not in trouble. No-one has been pushed into a defensive corner by accusations and the power of the group has shifted from the "bully leader" to the group as a whole, whose members withdraw consent for the behaviour to continue.

Each member of the group is then encouraged to suggest a way in which the victim could be helped to feel happier. These ideas are stated in the "I" language of intention. "I will walk to school with him." "I will ask him to sit with me at dinner." Ideas are owned by the group members and not imposed by the facilitator. She makes positive responses but she does not go on to extract a promise of improved behaviour.

Step six - leave it up to them.

The facilitator ends the meeting by passing over the responsibility to the group to solve the problem. No written record is made - it is left as a matter of trust. She thanks them, expresses confidence in a positive outcome and arranges to meet with them again to see how things are going.

Step seven - meet them again.

About a week later, the teacher discusses with each student, including the victim, how things have been going. This allows the teacher to monitor the bullying and keeps the young people involved in the process.

These meetings are with one group member at a time so that each can give a statement about his contribution without creating a competitive atmosphere. It does not matter if everyone has not kept to his intention, as long as the bullying has stopped.

The victim does not have to become the most popular person in school, just to be safe and happy.

The entire process showing the seven steps is available as a training video (Maines and Robinson, 1992).

What makes the process work?

Empathy and Altruism

When we first developed our approach, we were looking for a process that would bring about an empathic response in the bully and the rest of the group.

In the majority of cases this happens, and we have often heard words such as these:

> "*I knew we weren't being very nice but I never realised just how much it was affecting Michael.*"

In some cases the bully may not have any concern for the victim, but if some of the group understand the victim's pain, they often provide supportive strategies.

It may only take one or two people to be friendly to stop the feeling of isolation and pain of the victim.

Just one friend.

> *Before taking his life the boy wrote a message in the class diary, a portion of which I quote.*

> *"I decided to kill myself because day after day I go to school and only bad things happen. Nothing good ever happens to me. If the kids in my class could be in my shoes they would understand how I feel. If only they knew how I feel every day. Even in my dreams there are nothing but bad things.*
> *The only one I can talk to is the hamster, but the hamster can't speak back. Maybe my being born was a mistake... I can't stop the tears now. There was one, only one thing I wanted while I was alive, a friend I could talk to, really talk to from the heart. Just one friend like that, only one, was all I wanted."*

Yoshio (1985)

Shame

The perpetrators are not identified but they know who is responsible for the victim's distress. There is no stigmatising shame to make them likely to seek revenge but an internalised shame that is likely to help them change their behaviour.

Power

The intervention alters the dynamics of the group. Even if the bully does not want to change behaviour patterns, the rest of the group, with their statements of good intent, take the power away from the bully. He finds it very difficult to continue with the hurtful behaviour in the light of the supportive strategies provided by the rest of the group.

"I"-language of intent

Normal patterns of teacher language that are used to deal with inappropriate behaviour are described by Gordon (1974) as 'you' language:

> "*If you do this again.*"
> "*Why did you behave like that?*"
> "*Do you realise how serious this is?*"
> "*If this goes on you will be in serious trouble.*"

The pupils' helpful suggestions are stated in what we describe as the "I" - language of intent. They own the solution and there seems to be a significant shift in locus of control from external to internal.

> "*I will sit next to him in history.*"
> "*I'll invite him to my house.*"
> "*I will play football at breaktime with him.*"

This is far more likely to ensure that the strategies are implemented.

Problem-solving

The approach moves very quickly into problem-solving. By involving the young people in the process, it creates a more positive atmosphere than the traditional investigatory and adversarial methods.

Positive comments can be made about the suggestions as they

are put forward, and the group can be thanked at the end of the meeting for their help.

Monitoring and evaluation

The composition of the healthy group brings the problem out into the open; many more people have a knowledge of the problem and a commitment to do something about it.

The decision to see all those involved at the final stage changes the initial group into a series of individuals, all with their own responsibilities. Their unique contributions can be recognised, and they can leave feeling proud of this.

Evaluation

The No Blame Approach is sometimes challenged because there have been no research projects to evaluate its effectiveness. For example, Rigby (1996) writes, *"Hard evidence from unbiased evaluators of the method is notably lacking"* (p. 208). Yet this is true of most methods - and many claims of success are made which seem to have no sound statistical basis.

In the same book Rigby notes that the approach *"is likely to work better with younger children."* He gives no evidence in support of this view, which conflicts with much of the experience reported to us. We wonder what basis Rigby has for his suggestion.

It is irritating to read that there is "insufficient evidence" for our approach, when the Pikas Method of Shared Concern was used by only 12 teachers in the Sheffield research referred to below. Rigby notes some of the critiques of the method but then goes on to state:

> *"However, the method is understood best through participationι in workshops provided by Pikas himself. During his visit to ... Australia in 1995 the method was explored in some depth in his workshop, and the present account is based, in part, on the experience of attending one of these."* (p. 209)

We greatly admire the pioneering work of Pikas and hold him in the highest esteem, but feel that, if a researcher's participation in a workshop is sufficient to provide evidence in support of a method, then the accounts presented here may also have some validity.

Since we began training teachers in our approach, in November 1991, we have undertaken two separate evaluations of the usefulness of the programme from two perspectives:

- Does the distress of the victim reduce after the intervention?
- Do the users, mainly teachers, find the programme easy to use?

Study one

The initial evaluation used a questionnaire and interview in June 1992 of teachers who had been trained in December 1991 and January 1992.

The results were as follows:

Primary school success rate	8/8
Secondary school success rate	47/49
Further Education success rate	2/2

where success is defined as when the teacher, having discussed the outcome with the victim, reports that the intervention was "helpful" or "very helpful".

Study two

The No Blame Approach is supported by a training video and workbooks (Maines and Robinson, 1992). A questionnaire was sent to 100 schools which had bought the materials. In order to collect useful data the survey form was quite long and this might explain the poor returns - only 13, which included one stating that the LEA did not participate in any data collection and one which was incomplete. Reports came from 2 middle, 1 junior and 8 secondary schools, covering 46 separate incidents.

In all instances, the approach was rated as successful (including one case where the intervention was repeated, as there was no immediate effect).

All eleven schools rated the approach positively: very good (3), positive (4), incredibly successful (1), very effective (1), very useful (2).

Ten schools reported an increase in the ability of staff to tackle bullying with confidence. Five schools involved parents in 16 of the interventions.

Consideration of these evaluations

There has been no attempt to compare these findings with data obtained from a control group, or a group for whom another intervention was used. We do not consider it ethical to encourage interventions, such as punishing the aggressors, which we believe would be significantly less helpful, or even harmful. Neither do we think it justifiable to use a control group. No adult faced with distressed young people should leave them unhelped just to see how many of them improve without any assistance. We believe that when young people ask for help, adults have a duty to respond in a way that they think will succeed, not to turn children into unwitting subjects for spurious research purposes.

The only type of intervention that might provide a satisfactory comparative group, because it is based on an appropriate philosophy, might be the Common Concern Method. (Pikas, 1989). The success of this method has been evaluated in the Sheffield Project (Smith and Sharp, 1994) and a 70% success rate is described. The two approaches have some similarities but the No Blame Approach does not require such an intensive training programme and is much less time-consuming to implement.

Another consideration might be that, since the victim is likely to disclose distress at a time of crisis, there might be a natural improvement regardless of any intervention. Whilst we acknowledge this to be a possibility, the idea that an adult might respond to the disclosure with just an assurance that "it will probably get better soon", would be unacceptable to most teachers and parents.

It is important to see this intervention as a part of a whole programme which includes strategies to reduce the frequency of bullying and which makes a clear statement to the staff, students and the community that bullying is taken seriously and is not acceptable. All must understand that the school community will not allow young people to suffer because of unkind behaviour by others. Whenever such behaviour occurs the group must accept the responsibility to put it right.

Many of our colleagues have tried out the No Blame Approach, and their reports are covered in some depth in the next chapter. We have now received numerous encouraging accounts of its success, a few of which are recorded below. Sometimes, slight modifications have been made to the process, either because the approach was not explained carefully enough, or because some changes seemed to suit the style of a particular teacher. For example, a primary school Head took the victim in to meet with the group of bullies (which was fine, as the victim in question was robust enough and willing to speak for himself).

A primary school headteacher:

I found the strategy quite difficult in terms of my own attitudes - resisting the temptation to blame and tell off bullies does not come easily! The children took it all in their stride and relationships were not damaged by the process - no recriminations were observed, as no one had "got into trouble". In terms of time expended, the process was very economical - no more than an hour being spent on it in total - and yet the results have been quite staggering. There has been no recurrence of the problem whatsoever, and about six months have passed now. It seems to have been about the nearest thing possible to a "Magic Aspirin" for bullying!

A comprehensive school deputy head:

Each time the empathy method has been used it has worked. It takes time, but no more so than collating individual statements from pupils. Also, we have had no parental comeback either in terms of positive or negative feedback. It would appear that everyone just feels relieved!

A parent of a nine-year-old boy:

My boy was a victim of school bullying, and when he came home he used to behave in a very nasty way towards his younger brother - as though he was taking it out on someone weaker. The school used the No Blame Approach and things changed for my son. Now he is happy to go into school and he is also much nicer to be with at home. I am really in favour of this method and I don't think punishing the bullies would have worked as well.

Questions People Ask

You are not seen to be taking strong action - what will parents, pupils and colleagues think?

A school which has a clear written policy which sets out its anti-bullying procedures is not likely to incur disapproval from the community. In our experience, dissatisfaction arises when teachers do not take parental complaints seriously or when they respond by blaming the victim: "It's six of one and half a dozen of the other", "She doesn't do much to help herself."

We have explained the No Blame Approach at several parents' meetings, and reactions have been very positive. Parents of victims do sometimes feel angry, or want revenge, but when they are confident that action will be taken, we find that they agree that the most important thing is to stop the bullying.

What do you do if there is a serious incident of violence?

When a pupil is seriously assaulted by another then the usual sanctions must be applied, even calling the police if that is appropriate. The No Blame Approach can still be used as well, since there is no need to discuss the particular incident of violence. What should be addressed is the misery of the victim and how that might be alleviated.

Surely you need to know exactly what went on?

It is only necessary to know that bullying is happening and to have the names of the young people involved. Any attempts to take accurate accounts about the events are likely to stir up further disputes, to increase hostility towards the victims and to waste a lot of time, because the "truth" may be hard to find and may vary from one person's perspective to another's. Bullying is a complex process and you are not likely to discover all the ramifications, and certainly not all the causes, by questioning the participants.

What if only one bully is involved?

We believe that it is very rare that bullying takes place in real isolation - there is nearly always some knowledge and even consent from a group, even if they disapprove and refuse to join in. Secret bullying of one person by another is rare and hard to discover, but if it is revealed then the No Blame Approach might still be tried. A peer group could be given the opportunity to help put things right, even if they have not been involved in the unhappiness.

It might be worth considering whether the kinds of interventions used on child-protection programmes would be helpful for these situations, since they may apply to abuse of an individual by another who is not a member of the peer group.

What if the bully is seriously disturbed?

Pupils with seriously maladaptive behaviours should be helped in the usual ways. The No Blame Approach is a method that can be used to stop bullying, not to treat pathology. Any individual who is involved in this process may be offered other additional interventions or be referred for specialist advice as necessary.

What about victims who provoke bullying? Why can't we help the victim directly?

Some victims may display behaviours which appear to encourage bullying from their peers. Young people who have poor social and friendship skills, or who are very unassertive, can be offered help and support in order to learn appropriate social interaction - although this should not be taken to imply that they are responsible for dealing with the bullying by themselves.

When the group convenes to discuss the plight of the victim, someone may suggest that he or she is encouraged to behave in a different way. "We could ask her to stop..." That is fine as long as the group takes the responsibility to help her, and the changes are within her ability.

What do we tell the parents?

If anyone is hurting more than the victim it is likely to be the parents who may present, initially, as angry, blameful and needing revenge. When they are allowed to express these feelings, without denial or resistance on the part of the listener, we have almost always found that it is possible to reach agreement about the first priority... everyone wants the bullying to stop. In all but two cases from a collection of hundreds of accounts, the parents have at least agreed that the school could try the No Blame Approach.

We suggest that:
- Parents and pupils all receive and understand the school policy.
- Parents are told that, when incidents are reported or observed, the No Blame Approach will be used.
- Not every incident will be reported to all parents, just as not every incident of other "difficulties" such as lateness or forgetting homework, is reported.
- The school will always contact parents if there are significant concerns about behaviour or well being.
- Parents are encouraged to discuss any worries they might have, with a promise that they will be heard.

Conclusion

Bullying is a serious problem, which spoils the lives and learning of a significant number of young people in schools. It is time to stop collecting data on its frequency. It occurs in all schools. Preventive approaches will reduce it but it will still happen and teachers need to know how to deal with it when it does.

The No Blame Approach seems almost too simple and it may be hard for some teachers to let go of the traditional ways of dealing with bullying - such as interrogation and punishment. However, the students and parents tell us that what they care about is that the behaviour stops. The No Blame Approach achieves just that.

Since 1997 some independent evidence for the effectiveness of the approach was published (Young, S .1998). She reports on a two-year project in Kingston upon Hull where the Special Educational Needs Support Service offered schools advice and support for individual referrals for bullying incidents. During two years the service dealt with over 80 referrals that required active involvement beyond advice over the phone. She describes the cases as being serious,

"By the very nature of the referral process, the complaints tend to be serious - indeed the police may have been involved, there may have been a medical referral, the problem may have been going on for years and the child may be absent from school."

The intervention used was a No Blame Approach with minor modifications. It was used in 55 cases (over 70% of referrals) and the referrals were predominantly from primary schools.

Young (1998) writes,

"The approach has been successful in the great majority of cases - to be precise the bullying stopped completely or the victim no longer felt in need of support."

Of the 51 primary cases, there was immediate success in 40 (80%), success delayed in 7 (14%) where the intervention had to be continued after the first meeting and limited success 3 (6%) where the victim continued to mention incidents that bothered him/her, although there had been considerable improvement. One case was not completed because the child was excluded. Of the four referrals from secondary schools, two were of immediate success and the other two could not be completed as the pupils had left the school.

Young states,

"The confidence of Maines and Robinson has been substantiated in our experience, so much so that now SENSS advises the schools to adopt this approach, unless there are compelling and usually obvious reasons why it would not be appropriate."

Chapter 9

Variations on a theme:
101 ways to use the approach

Jane, one of our colleagues, has been using the No Blame Approach since 1992. In this chapter she describes some strategies that she has found helpful.

As with all documented methods of dealing with incidents of unacceptable behaviour, we have to be prepared to modify the approach to meet the needs of the individual situation.

Only about half of the cases of bullying I have handled, using the No Blame Approach, have followed the procedure as explained previously. Many require adaptation or, in a few cases, a repeat meeting. As a practitioner of five years' standing, I hope this chapter will provide you with some of the tricks of the trade and guidelines for incidents that do not follow the normal pattern of events.

The advice has been broken down into the stages involved in the No Blame Approach, followed by some specific case studies and adaptations.

Meeting with the victim.

Regardless of how you have come to hear about the bullying behaviour, you will need to speak to the victim - either alone or with a friend or parent. Allow enough time for this interview. If the need is not immediate, then arrange a time that is convenient for all involved.

Ask if you can take notes during the meeting, as they will help you later when you meet with the group. Check whether there are any details the victim does not wish to be shared. Remember that students who are unable to express themselves clearly may find it easier to do a drawing or tell a story.

How does the victim choose the group?

This needs to be done carefully so that there are equal numbers of bullies, watchers and friends of the victim. For "isolated" victims, the group should include those with whom the victim would like to be friends (see case study 1). If the group is multicultural, ensure that the numbers of bullies, friends and watchers are balanced. The watchers should be popular and respected students who can influence their peers in a positive way.

In discussion with the victim, establish how quickly you need to convene the group. Is it essential, for the safety of the victim, that you meet immediately, or can it wait until you do not need to get cover for your lesson?

How do you establish communication with the victim so that you know that the meeting has been successful?

For the victim's, and your, reassurance there needs to be regular feedback so you know that the behaviour has stopped. You must agree that the victim will tell you immediately if things are not going well after the meeting with the group.

Many students readily communicate their happiness that things are much better for them, or that there is still room for improvement. In a larger school, you may not see the student in a situation where you can ask without peers being present. I have established a signing system. We identify a 'raised eyebrow' or 'thumbs up' sign so I can know whether further intervention is required or things are going well. These messages can be conveyed to me as I walk around the school and peers need not be aware. 'Are you OK?' is not the right question to ask people who need to build their self-esteem or confidence. An agreed sign, though, can be read quickly and enables a meeting to be arranged if necessary.

Contacting parents

If parents are not aware that their son or daughter is being bullied, then it is at this point that you may contact them to explain what you are doing to help alleviate the problem. I feel that a meeting or telephone call is easier than a letter. Remember that if they are unaware what the No Blame Approach is you will have to explain to them what you will be doing to help. It may be useful to send them a copy of the parents' leaflet (Maines and Robinson 1995).

The meeting with the students

After you have carefully chosen the group, they need to be told of the meeting. If you collect the group yourself, ensure that no explanation is given of why you are meeting until you are together. If messages are sent via the registers, check that all the students you need are in school; the key characters must be present.

When I first started using the No Blame Approach I was the only member of staff who used it and if I called for students they immediately knew why. I recommend that several staff should be trained, so that you do not get labelled!

How do you start the meeting?

"We are here to help X who is feeling ... "

Remember to stick to feelings that you agreed could be shared. As you start explaining the victim's feelings I can guarantee that nine times out of ten someone will say, 'But it wasn't me!' or 'She did it to me first!' At this point, you need to say that you have not said that anyone did anything to anyone else, and no blame has been apportioned to anyone. Repeat that you have asked them to come along as you are sure that they can help X feel a lot happier.

Common responses are:

"But he/she is so annoying." - see case study 1.

"We did not realise..." - see case study 2.

"He/she does not seem to mind." - explain that the person does mind and may have been covering it up well, but we still need to help so they can feel happier.

"He/she did it to me first." - remind the group that we are not here to discuss actions but feelings. You can talk to that student afterwards, if you suspect that he or she, too, may be suffering from bullying.

Solutions:
These are usually incredibly simple. Students may need prompting, but once they have some ideas from you they will soon come up with ideas of their own. For example:
"Ask X to sit with us."
"Walk to school with X."
"Ask my friends to stop being nasty to X."
"Ignore X"s annoying habits."
"Ask X to join in with our games."
"Just not speak to X."

Check that they know what they are going to do, but do not record their responses. Arrange a time for individual meetings so that you can see how things are going.

What if they do not offer solutions?
I have never experienced a complete refusal to offer ideas, but there is sometimes reluctance, especially if the victim has annoying habits or is, in some way, provoking the hostile behaviour. You must reiterate that you need to help the victim feel

happier, which may lead to a change in the victim's behaviour. As a group they can help, as they have the support of each other. (See case study 1.)

As an alternative you can ask if any of the group have been bullied, or take them back to PSE work you have done on bullying and the effects it can have on people. Try to raise the empathy of the group.

If the ideas have been slow in coming forward, I recommend an early meeting with the victim to ensure that the behaviours have stopped. If there is still a problem, then a second group may need to be convened with different students.

Who needs to know that you have had the meeting?

Parents have already been contacted, so you now need to inform tutors or class teachers. If the bullying was occurring at breaktimes, then ask duty staff in the playground, or dinner supervisors, to keep a watch, too.

Feedback

During the intervening time you will have seen the students around school and established how things are going. If the behaviour has improved, then the feedback discussion with individuals need only be brief. Remember to thank the group for helping. If things are not any better then you will probably have heard by now! If there is partial improvement, then encourage the students to keep their offers of help going and enrol some other students into the group.

If there is no change then a second meeting must be called and further suggestions put forward. A change of group members could help.

Case study 1 - an isolated student

Laura was in year 7 and had extreme difficulties settling in at secondary school. She had not attended much during the primary years and had not moved up to secondary school with any particular friends. She found it difficult to work in groups and was feeling very left-out and unhappy.

Her mother contacted me and I met with Laura to discuss the problem. She acknowledged that she found if difficult having to share and work with others. She appreciated that she had some annoying habits and wanted to know what they were so she could change as well as the group having to accept her.

I taught the group but did not know them very well, as it was near to the beginning of the school year. The group included all the confident girls with whom Laura wanted to become friends. We met and ideas were put forward. They also responded to Laura's question as to what her annoying habits were. I explained that many of these were due to the fact that she had been taught at home and was not used to working in a group. We established some strategies that they could all use.

For a few days, things went well but it did not last for long and Laura slowly became isolated again. At our second meeting I explained to Laura, who was not convinced that this approach was going to work, that I thought we had not chosen the right group. It was instinct that led Laura to the popular group in the class rather than the more unassuming girls who would fit in with her character and interests more readily. I asked Laura who she would invite to a party if she were to have one so she would choose a different group.

When I met with the second group one of the girls asked why Laura had chosen them, I explained about the suggestion of who she would invite to a party. At this Sarah responded, 'Oh, isn't that nice!' and the meeting went extremely well and a picnic and sleepover were already being planned as we left the room.

Laura, now in year 9, is one of the more confident students and her attendance and academic progress have improved dramatically.

Hint:

In cases of isolation, choose the students who would relate well to the victim and not necessarily the ones that the victim would, ideally, like to be friends with.

Case study 2 - "We did not realise"

The incident involved a girl in Year 8 who was very attractive, able, musical and gave the impression that everything was all right. However, unbeknown to the staff and her peers, this was far from the case.

Eventually Nadine's parents contacted the school and explained that she was extremely unhappy at home and was beginning to say that she was too unwell to come to school. Nadine explained to me how unhappy she was; although the girls were trying to include her, she felt that she was always the odd one out. We chose the group carefully and I met with them.

The response was one of shock, "But Nadine is always so confident and good at everything - we had no idea she felt like this." *It is cases like this that contradict the stereotypical view of "victims" and "bullies". The ideas were spontaneous and easy to implement and other suggestions were put forward to help Nadine. Within a few weeks, she had a large circle of friends.*

Hint:
   Do not assume that the confident students, who may appear not to want friends, are happy with their situations. Some students do not show their unhappiness at school but it manifests itself in different behaviours at home. If parents contact you about uncharacteristic behaviour that they are seeing, speak to the student and establish whether bullying could be the problem.

The victim does not want to do anything about it.
   If students insist that what happens is not, in their eyes, serious bullying, establish that if there is any repeat of the behaviour then you need to know immediately. Tell the students that you will inform their parents and watch carefully to ensure that things are all right.
   If a student obviously needs help, but is not happy about revealing names because, even after reassurance, he is frightened of retribution, ask him to speak to someone you have helped previously. I have a few students in school who have offered to speak to other victims in situations like these. A peer telling them that it does work is often a greater influence than a teacher.
   I have recently dealt with a student who was very unhappy about me revealing his name. He experienced lots of name-calling and took a long time to tell anyone. The group involved are known for their verbal unpleasantness to several students and to each other. We decided to honour his request as it was not only David who was experiencing the verbal abuse. He gave me a list of individuals and the year head and tutor added to it. As part of the PSE programme, I always ask students to complete an evaluation sheet. This checks up on their understanding and helps me to gauge how confident they are with the No Blame Approach. The questions are structured to enable me to talk to individuals or groups and discuss their responses. By referring to the students' replies I was able to start the group off by recalling their answers, in general terms, not specifically. The discussion went extremely well and led to questions as to whether certain behaviours could be construed as bullying. Knowing how David

was feeling, I was able to put forward his point of view, anonymously, and use that as the basis to decide whether the bullying behaviour was bullying in the eyes of the receiver or giver. The group went on to discuss the possibilities of having a "name-calling box", like a swear-box. The tutor is still working on that one!

Paul told me that he was being picked on, but felt that it was not serious enough to warrant a meeting; he did, however, want it to stop. Again, he was one of several victims of name-calling and minor harassment. We discussed the possibilities and, as it was very soon after the evaluation sheet had been completed, we decided to ask a few of the main protagonists to meet with me to discuss their responses to the questions. I met with the group, who all felt that the PSE input had had a very good effect on them and that they were definitely not hurting or insulting anyone by calling them names. I praised them for their positive approach and asked them to make sure that it continued and to let me know if they felt that anyone in the group needed a reminder about the effect of name-calling. Paul happily came to see me saying that all the unpleasant behaviours had stopped.

The victim wants to attend the meeting

Ranjit insisted on attending the meeting. As we talked to the group, the differences began to manifest themselves again. We returned to the issues of feelings but personal grievances continued to recur. After a long session the group agreed on behaviours that could be modified and stopped. During the follow-up meetings one of the support group, Linda, explained how she did not think the approach was very successful. The victim was much happier, however, and had re-established friendships with all the groups, including the girl who was not convinced with the approach. A few months later Linda asked if I could help her as she was being bullied by a group of boys. We worked together with a successful outcome. When I spoke to her afterwards I mentioned that she had not been convinced earlier. Linda explained that her friendship with Ranjit was now stronger and that maybe her initial response had been wrong.

Just involving two students

A year 11 boy, Michael, hit out at another student, Earl. When questioned, Michael explained that Earl had been calling him gay for months. Other students were involved, but he was the main perpetrator. The teacher dealing with the situation decided just to talk to the two boys individually. Michael explained that he needed to wear glasses, as his eyesight was extremely poor. After games lessons, when he had not yet collected his glasses from the PE teacher, he had to establish where all his clothes were in the changing rooms. In order to do this, he needed to grope around and had, on occasion, touched other people. This had been misconstrued as him being gay. It was only by talking to Michael that his view of the situation could be understood. The member of staff next talked to Earl, who appreciated Michael's predicament. After I had spoken to the two boys separately, they were asked to meet together so the reason could be explained. Earl and Michael shook hands and Earl promised to tell the other lads and arranged to help Michael sort out his clothes after PE lessons.

The main group have sorted it out, but the hangers-on miss their fun.

I am sure you are familiar with this scenario: Two good friends, A and B, have an argument and walk off in a huff. A goes up to classmate C and has a bit of a moan about B. C meets D (the class stirrer) and says that A and B have had an argument and, "you should hear what A is saying about B", elaborating on the story to make it sound more interesting.

In the meantime A and B have got back together again.

Later, D goes up to B and says that A has been saying horrible things about him/her and he/she should have nothing to do with A. B and A then fall out and A is bullied by the three of them.

You can play this situation in several different ways. I usually get the two friends, A and B, together and establish how much trust there is between them. The other two are then included in the group and it is explained to them how much their behaviour has affected A and B.

This is such a common situation that I endeavour to get some role play activities in PSE or assemblies so the students can see how upsetting and futile their attempts at breaking up friendships can be.

When those on the periphery really cause the problems.

Boy and girl friend, Rhys and Natalie, split up. Their "friends" got involved and kept claiming that Natalie was saying horrible things about Rhys, then they wrote nasty letters and made telephone calls. Similar reports came back to Natalie about Rhys. They tried to ignore it but eventually they challenged each other and Rhys ended up physically abusing Natalie. The situation then involved teachers who, up until then, had been unaware of the problem.

I used the No Blame Approach very successfully with the students in this case, despite Rhys having been suspended for a couple of days because of the attack. Both of them had been the victims of bullying by their peers and so I spoke to them individually and then met with some of their friends to explain the situation and ask for their help. Rhys and Natalie, although not boy and girl friend, still respected each other and did not wish the behaviour of others to impinge on their relationship. For a few days, things went quite well, Rhys and Natalie getting on together and close friends being supportive.

Some of those on the periphery were obviously missing the entertainment they had had at the others' expense and pointed them out to each other: "That's Natalie, who was hit by Rhys", and other such provocative comments. Natalie and her mother came to see me, feeling that the No Blame Approach had not worked as far as the wider group was concerned. Natalie did not wish further meetings to be held but did want something to be done, so we negotiated an assembly. I was to talk to the students about bullying generally and the effects it had on people, and would mention the No Blame Approach and how successful it was with those directly involved. However we, as onlookers, were to remember that we too had a role and ensure that we should not incite further unpleasantness by getting involved in something that is not pertinent to us or by rekindling past unpleasantness that has been resolved. For Natalie and Rhys, the comments stopped. I did not mention any names or incidents in assembly but the impact the initial incident had had on the group was sufficient for them all to know what my message meant.

The last two incidents illustrate the need for regular input, using assembly, tutorial time, PSE, on the rights of the student. This will emphasise the importance of feelings and empathy for those directly involved in any incident. The role of the bystanders is so important and yet with most other ways of dealing with bullying they are not considered to be significant enough to play a part in helping.

Jane Sleigh

Chapter 10

Accounts from colleagues

Earlier we mentioned our attempts to evaluate our approach systematically. There are other means of evaluation, of course, including the first-hand accounts of people who have used the approach. Clearly, these might not be considered "objective" - to which we would say that any "bias" results from people's success with the method. As professionals they would not change their approaches unless they were convinced that the No Blame Approach was better than their previous attempts to stop bullying.

We are accused of providing no independent evaluation of our work. This raises the interesting question of what would actually count as independent. Here are some accounts, provided by a variety of people with no axe to grind, who give their opinions of the No Blame Approach.

The BBC

A BBC Director/Producer, who was investigating bullying for the BBC 2 Bullying Season (26 to 31 August 1997), came to discuss our approach. After further research, he asked to observe a training session, and came to Nottingham for a No Blame training day. As a result of this, we were then asked to train the whole staff of one school, and the BBC followed the school's progress made in implementing the approach. The filming culminated in a 40-minute programme (I just want it to stop - 27 August 1997), which examined three bullying incidents, all of which had positive outcomes.

Over six months I had to research, direct and produce three films for BBC2's Bully Season. Taking on what used to be three different roles was a lot of work, but gave me the opportunity to get completely absorbed in the subject-matter. It turned out to be a fascinating and rewarding experience. As the programmes were funded by BBC Education, the brief was to produce something which was informative and also helpful, not something you might normally associate with most television.

However, the temptation was to be drawn towards the more dramatic end of the anti-bullying spectrum, bully courts, exclusion etc. on the grounds that this would be good TV. Once I realised how redundant most punishment-based strategies were, I concentrated on "listening" techniques like Circle Time and No Blame.

What attracted me most to No Blame was firstly, that it appeared to work, and secondly, that it required most new practi-

tioners to undergo a kind of conversion. Old prejudices had to be abandoned - it was a new way of seeing things which could change all the parties involved. Perhaps most of all it was supportive, an element often sorely lacking in schools.

As a result, our programmes made no attempt to offer a "balanced" view; we wholeheartedly recommended schools to adopt No Blame and parents to press for its introduction. It was something we never regretted.

Ian Pye (BBC-TV)

A Teacher Adviser's Perspective.

As a teacher adviser working with all levels of school staff in mainstream and special schools, I became aware of the growing importance of helping schools to put in place effective systems for responding to bullying. Although bullying is still an abiding problem, that has often been seen as an inevitable part of childhood, there is now a climate of concern about addressing bullying in school and in the workplace. Until recently, schools have held back on publicly taking action on bullying for fear of being labelled as having problems. Because of open enrolment and delegated budgets no-one wished to risk the possible consequences of such labelling. However, many schools have tackled this difficulty by pointing out that all schools, at some time, will have to deal with bullying and, therefore, need to have clear, effective systems in place.

Historically, bullying has been dealt with by punishing the bullies. Retribution may have some value, but when dealing with bullying we need to keep an open mind about the impact and effectiveness of punishing bullies. Might punishment make it worse, risking further alienation of the child? This is not to say that bullying behaviour should be ignored or condoned. In addition to this consideration, there is research evidence to show that some youngsters are resistant to punishment (Davies J.G.V. and Maliphant, R. 1974). The value of retribution in such cases may only be the satisfaction of injured parties who believe in its value. It is also widely recognised by teachers that punishment, whilst it has some deterrent value, does not show children what to do; it concentrates on the negative, what not to do. This presents difficulties for those children for whom bullying is learnt behaviour and is "a way of life" - punishment alone is not likely to cure the problem.

What, then, can we do? It is essential to deal with incidents of bullying as they occur, but, if that is the only response, it is rather like fire-fighting, lurching from crisis to crisis - of marginal value in the long run. Substantial, longer-term intervention is required to minimise the occurrence of bullying.

The effective management of responding to bullying is a priority. This requires essential elements of personal and social education. Further, it is a whole-school issue, which also involves working with parents. The longer-term implications for the personal and social education of children who bully and for their victims are evident. The aims of education are the same for all children, and in terms of personal and social education, they are personal autonomy (self-determination), self-acceptance and social competence. Personal responsibility and empathy are encouraged by raising the awareness of all the children about the nature of bullying and, in particular, the extent to which children are hurt by it. This also diminishes the likelihood of passive spectators or acolytes of the bully taking no action. The raised awareness about bullying is likely to reduce support for bullies, and should also encourage children to report bullying. It thereby informs children by helping them to make considered decisions and to take responsibility for their actions, both by not supporting the bully and by telling. The increased awareness is part of helping them to learn about the needs and rights of other people - an important aspect of social competence.

In the short term, it is unreasonable to expect victimised children to do much to change their situation. If they knew how to, they would have already taken action. Since bullying often has very damaging effects on the victim, specialist help may be required and should not be overlooked or marginalised in our efforts to deal with the bully. Over time it may be possible to help bullied children to become assertive so that they have some skills to deal with less severe types of bullying. The most reassuring knowledge for children who have been bullied is that the school will take action on their behalf and stop the bullying.

A major aspiration in working with children who bully will be to prevent the behaviour recurring and to move the children forward in their personal growth. An important strategy in this regard is to provide the opportunity for reparation. When we have done something wrong it is not the end of the world, it is possible to "put it right" with the injured party. An early stage in this process is for the bullied children to acknowledge their own bad feelings about what they have done and to discuss ways of putting it right. Then, to provide support in putting the intentions into action. In the longer term, the state of a bullying child's self-esteem will need to be addressed. Children who bully usually have negative self-esteem. Sometimes this is difficult to discern as it may be covered by a front of bravado or outward confidence. The bullying behaviour is likely to be driven by "deficit" needs for recognition, admiration and power.

My work with schools involved investigating many of the published packs on bullying to identify the most useful suggestions. Among them were many practical and persuasive ideas. I was interested in the No Blame Approach for a number of reasons:

- Its sheer economy. It is one solution to many problems and therefore economical of teacher time and effort.
- It provides an immediate response to the situation; peers, parents and others can see that something has been done.
- It fosters empathy, raising awareness of the scale of the victim's hurt, with the peers who may have been bystanders or supporters of the bully. By raising awareness in this way, it reduces the support for the bully.
- It provides an opportunity for children to help to make the bullied child feel better, thereby enabling children to take responsibility for their own actions.
- It engages the good-will of the bystanders, by focusing on how to help the victim, rather than on punishing the bully.
- It engages the group in solving the problem faced by the victim; because they have ownership of the problem, they have greater investment and commitment in carrying out the solution.

In conclusion, the No Blame Approach is a neat, concise, effective system that deals both with the short- and the longer-term responses to bullying, providing opportunities for learning that lead to personal and social growth. In this respect, I see the No Blame Approach as a "giant above the rest" among packs to deal with bullying.

Pat Jacques,

An Educational Psychologist who uses Two Methods
Pragmatics versus Therapy: The No Blame Approach and the Method of Shared Concern.

Methods of resolving bullying situations that do not seek to *apportion blame, find the truth or exact a punishment are rapidly finding favour amongst teachers and educational psychologists. The simple reason is that in the majority of cases the specific situation of bullying is stopped. The two main non-punitive methods are the No Blame Approach and the Pikas Method of Shared Concern. At first glance there appears to be very little significant difference between these approaches. Both explicitly warn the practitioner against seeking out the "truth" of the situation. Both encourage the victims to voice their feelings about the bullying situation. Finally, both methods accept that bullying is part of a normal range of behaviours and in the majority of cases, it is both inappropriate and unproductive to punish those who are doing the bullying.*

There are, however, more subtle differences between the two methods other than the order in which one sees bullies and victims. I believe that the main strength of the No Blame Approach is that it is a pragmatic method that makes it very clear to those who are doing the bullying that their activities have been "rumbled". Without apportioning any blame, it gives those involved a chance to make amends without losing face in front of their peer group. My experience is that when the bullies are encouraged to give suggestions as to how they can change and resolve the situation, they often make grand and too friendly suggestions as how they can help the victim. Suggestions such as "I will share my sweets with him" or "I will call for him on the way to school" are common. In reality, such suggestions are seldom followed through, but the bullies generally leave the victim alone to the obvious relief of the victim and his or her parents. It is unlikely that any psychological transformation has taken place on the part of the bullies and in few cases has the victim been encouraged to consider the effects of their own behaviour. Neither of these factors should be seen as a criticism of the No Blame Approach, as, in my experience, and in that of many of my colleagues the approach has been extremely successful. Both teachers and psychologists find its uncomplicated process and philosophy appealing and its effectiveness can be demonstrated in all but the most complex of bullying situations.

So, is there really a need for another similar non-punitive, non-blaming approach to tackling bullying, especially when the author of this approach generally recommends its use by only those who have some experience of counselling or therapeutic work with children? Perhaps there would be a need if one approach claimed a greater degree of effectiveness or stated that there were certain types of bullying situations that only responded to one particular type of intervention. My understanding is that neither of the approaches makes such extravagant claims and it is likely that many of those practitioners who are aware of both are happy to interchange between the two approaches.

As I have gained more experience as a facilitator in the resolution of bullying situations, I have begun to realise that I do tend to favour the more overtly therapeutic "Method of Shared Concern" when dealing with an all too common but potentially very difficult situation, that of the "provocative victim". The majority of classroom teachers are able to readily identify such children - those who appear to go out of their way to provoke hostility both in adults and in other children. Many provocative victims continue to associate with a group even though they are often the butt of jokes, name-calling and even physical aggression. In such cases I feel that it is necessary to mediate a change in the victim's behaviour as well as demonstrating to the bullying group that they can be part of the solution to a problem that they see is not entirely of their making.

In both the No Blame Approach and in the Method of Shared Concern, it is essential to put from one's mind the notion that one party in the bullying situation is wholly guilty and one is wholly innocent. This is particularly true in the case of the provocative victim. In this situation, the teacher or psychologist is not merely attempting to show the bullies that activities are now known to adults and that they have the chance to make amends without being punished. They also need to help the victim to explore how his behaviour is contributing to the unhappy state of affairs whilst at the same time demonstrating to the bullies, without condoning their activities, that they are justified in feeling annoyed at the victim for seeking out their attention even when they have made it clear that his behaviour is irritating. Interviews with both the bullies and victim demand considerable listening skills and demonstrations of empathy to both sides. One also needs to be highly attuned to when to move the discussion forward to suggestions of how both parties can change their behaviour to a position of mutual tolerance.

The Method of Shared Concern highlights the necessity of the final meeting. This meeting is potentially the most difficult part of the process but is essential where a provocative victim is involved. It is extremely important to prepare both the bullies and victim carefully, and it should be stressed that the meeting is *a way of cementing the positive actions that have arisen from the earlier meetings. Of equal importance, however, is the need to allow both sides the freedom to express their annoyance and frustration at the other party's behaviour. This final session is often daunting for inexperienced practitioners and can sometimes appear to be an arena for the airing of old quarrels and rancour. It is, however, an essential part of the "therapeutic" process and can demand counselling skills of the highest order from the practitioner. It is, of course, essential that both the victim and bullies are guided from the stage of recriminations towards the idea that both parties can live together and then on to a shared understanding of the practicalities of making this happen.*

Perhaps these different approaches to dealing with the problems of bullying should be seen as parts of a tool-kit and the decision as to which is the appropriate tool for that particular problem should be left to the individual. My own anecdotal evidence suggests that both methods work well in most cases. The straightforward nature of the No Blame Approach allows it to be readily passed on to colleagues in many different professions whereas the Method of Shared Concern demands a greater awareness of the psychological processes occurring between the bully, victim and "therapist". Some teachers feel uncomfortable working in such areas and are happier to pass on the more complex difficulties to those with greater experience and training. I hope that those who have this experience and training continue to be allowed the time to work with children and families caught up in the misery of bullying.

Richard Gilham

Getting rid of blame and punishment
Primary School Deputy Head

Two years ago I was given the responsibility for developing Lakes Primary School's policy for Behaviour, Discipline and Bullying and started to find out more about the issues involved. I was, therefore, quite susceptible to the message coming at me from an unsolicited mailshot that proclaimed, "Michael's being bullied. Here's what to do." I had a vague memory of the same message from months earlier when I had quickly grasped the opportunity to reduce my volume of paperwork by throwing the leaflet in the bin. This time my response was more positive.

A few weeks later a colleague and I were heading off to Durham University to spend our Saturday finding out more about the No Blame Approach. As we drove along I reflected on the many hours, over the years, that I had spent trying (with varying degrees of success and failure) to resolve instances of bullying. I was quite intrigued by the title of No Blame and the idea that someone could claim to have the answer to this problem. Previously, I had always tried to impress upon the culprit(s) the seriousness of their actions and the harm they had done to another person. I thought that "getting to the bottom of it" was essential if I was to ensure that the punishments meted out were fair and deserved. The consequences of getting it wrong were numerous, complicated, time-consuming and usually stressful for all involved. Even when I got it right, though, the process was nearly as stressful, and far from straightforward.

By lunchtime I was beginning to realise how many of my strategies and actions were actually helping to undermine what I was trying to achieve, although there were many teachers on the course who appeared to be much more resistant than I to considering the effectiveness of what they were doing. During the afternoon, the group was presented with the No Blame model and it became crystal clear to me that channelling my efforts into blame and punishment was counterproductive. Taking these two issues out of the process would enable me to deal with a bullying problem in a way that was consistent with how I normally interact with children. It offered me the scope to work in a problem-solving and supportive way.

I drove home full of enthusiasm about how I could work with children in order to resolve bullying, and wondered when I would be able to put the theory to the test. It wasn't a very long wait.

Four o'clock on a Friday afternoon: "Excuse me, Mr. Evans. Can I have a word with you? Our Mark is being bullied and I'd like it stopped."

I knew exactly what I was going to do and how I was going to do it. In a similar situation a month earlier I would have felt angry that Mark had been bullied and very frustrated that there was next to nothing I could do until Monday morning. Then I would start the week by embarking on a complicated and drawn-out process involving investigation, accusation, counter-accusation, cover-up, punishment and, probably, quite a few emotional meetings with parents. What a way to start the weekend! Instead, I invited Mark's mother into my room and we sat down while I listened to her describe what had happened and then explained how I was going to sort out the problem.

I asked her how Mark felt about the situation, and then explained that it would be very helpful if he could come to school with a written account of his feelings about the situation and how it had affected his life. Mark, 8 years old and not really able to express his ideas in writing very well, arrived at school the following Monday with a letter written for him by his aunt. It explained how his best friend was now his tormentor and that some of his other friends were part of the problem. He was isolated, having nightmares and suffering from asthma attacks.

I spent 10 minutes talking to him about this and asked who he thought I should speak to in order to stop the bullying. The group of six children included two who were still "nice" friends. Mark agreed that I could read his letter to the group. At morning break, I asked the six children to come and see me because there was a serious problem and I needed their help to resolve it. I explained that I was going to read them a letter from Mark. I also explained that the letter named one person and said to that particular boy that he should just listen and remember that he was there, like everyone else, because I needed their help to make Mark's life better.

The response I got as I read the letter was typical of what has happened on nearly every occasion since that time. Half way through reading the letter the "best friend" bully started crying. He realised and understood the full impact of what he had done to Mark. The rest was very easy (just follow the remaining steps of the No Blame approach) and Mark has been happy ever since. He still gives me the thumbs up (everything is fine) sign whenever he sees me around school.

I continued to try the No Blame approach for a little longer. As the Deputy Head in the school, parents seemed to come to me with the "serious" problems. Each time I worked through the seven steps and explained to the class teacher what I was doing and why. The No Blame Approach has helped me to resolve quickly and successfully every instance of bullying that I have been involved with since November 1993.

The next step with the policy development was how to secure a common approach to dealing with bullying. The staff agreed to commit two Professional Development days to working with George Robinson on the issues of raising self-esteem, using punishments positively, the No Blame Approach and how we could create a school environment where misbehaviour and bullying would be minimised. At the end of our two days, the staff were unanimous in adopting the No Blame Approach as our common strategy for dealing with bullying.

We also had a wide range of ideas to minimise bullying behaviour. In pursuit of these ideas, I became more aware of how the school grounds can have quite a dramatic affect upon the behaviour of children. After attending a "Learning Through Landscapes" conference and discovering how school grounds could be developed, the staff, children and parents became involved in planning for a better playtime.

We now have a plan for the development of the school grounds and have already converted one large quadrangle into a quiet retreat, complete with pond, marshes, log seats, picnic tables, shrubs and flowers. The children demonstrate a proud ownership of the area and are very enthusiastic in watering the plants and weeding the beds. One boy, who was admitted to school a few years ago as a difficult and insular 8 year old, recently spent a busy weekend with his friend baking cakes so that he could pay for an outdoor tap to enable other children to water the plants without sloshing water over the cloakroom floors.

It seems to me that the children have quickly accepted greater responsibility for their own environment. They asked for their own noticeboard to go up in our "patio" area and there are frequent requests from children for permission to do one thing or the other in order to raise money to continue the developments.

Two years later I know that for me there is no other way. The school is gradually working towards creating the sort of environment that interests and stimulates young children, provides "safe" areas, and is leading towards a greater use of the school grounds as an outdoor classroom.

Meanwhile, the main issue that promoted these changes is still a high priority. Parents have been invited into school so that the No Blame Approach can be presented and explained. From my experience, the only thing that parents are interested in when their child is being bullied is that it is stopped and their child is happy. I have recently asked some parents whose children have been the victims of bullying, to come along and give their impression of the No Blame Approach. Their support has been invaluable.

The most recent instance of bullying came to light when Anne's father asked if he could see me as he had discovered that his daughter had truanted because she had been too frightened to come to school. Anne (aged 11) is conscientious and takes school seriously and had spent the entire day in the local library, as she wanted to be in a safe place. He explained how two girls had threatened his daughter with a knife and that they had used the knife to cut off a small amount of Anne's hair. He had been unable to persuade Anne to come to school. The incident had happened outside of school hours and although one of the girls was in Anne's class, the other attended a different school.

Anne's father was undecided about whether he should go to the police. I explained that I shared his view that this was a serious issue and outlined how I would deal with the problem. I said that he might wish to see how things worked out before deciding to go to the police but that he should make his own decision on that matter. An hour later he returned with Anne so that we could record her feelings and establish which children I should talk to. They both went home and I met a group of girls at breaktime.

Once again, the bully broke down in tears before I had finished explaining how Anne had been so scared that she had truanted. The group made a number of suggestions as to how they could support Anne. One of the girls suggested they spoke to her over the phone to tell her that everything would be all right. I phoned her father and explained that the girls wanted to talk to Anne and that I thought it would be a good idea. He wasn't so sure but called his daughter to the phone. The first girl told Anne that everything was sorted. The second girl (the bully) took the phone told Anne, "It's OK, I won't stab you. We all want you back in school."

Later, Anne's mother told me how her daughter had been adamant about not going to school. However, as soon as Anne had put the phone down Anne had said, "I want to go school now." The change in attitude was instant. Anne's mother thought I had waved a magic wand.

Dealing with bullying is no longer a stressful and long drawn-out process but a quick and positive way of resolving problems. Occasionally I think about those resistant teachers I met two years ago in Durham and wonder how they are doing.

Chris Evans.

The No Blame Approach to Bullying at Colenso High School, Napier, New Zealand.
Deputy Principal:
Background: Colenso High School is a progressive, co-educational secondary school of 600 students (Years 9-13) in a small

provincial city, Napier, on the east coast of the North Island. The school, which emphasises school-wide processes, has developed innovative programmes to support student learning by focusing on self-esteem and providing practical organisational skills. In 1993, using the SCRE anti-bullying pack (1991 and 1993), the school, in collaboration with its community, agreed on an anti-bullying policy supported by a curriculum awareness-raising programme "Kia Kaha". The anti-bullying initiative was carefully monitored and its impact measured as part of a post-graduate study.

The results showed a dramatic decrease in the levels of bullying in the school but subsequent monitoring has shown that the impact and efficacy of the programme were limited and both enthusiasm for the programme, and willingness to counter bullying, dwindled during 1994.

Concern over this lack of sustained change led the Deputy Principal to apply for and be awarded a Nuffield Foundation Travel Bursary to study British approaches to bullying. February-April 1995 was spent in various parts of Britain looking at successful schemes.

The visit to Britain clearly showed that a Whole School Approach is the most successful way to reduce the levels of bullying in schools. The success of this approach was clearly demonstrated and reinforced during visits to Sheffield University, the Tayside "Anti-bullying" Team in Dundee and the Strathclyde Education Authority in Glasgow, as well as many schools. In the bulk of these visits, the school approach was focused on the development of a positive environment where bullying was not tolerated.

While vastly impressed by the commitment and success of these programmes in reducing bullying, there was little emphasis on solving the core problem of what to do with students who bullied.

No Blame Approach

During my visit to Bristol, I attended a training session at Patchway High School led by Barbara Maines and George Robinson who advocated the "No Blame Approach" for dealing with the inevitable cases of bullying. Their method filled in the missing element from the other programmes, with its problem-solving approach that dealt with changing the offending behaviour rather than attempting to change victims.

The application of the No Blame Approach

On my return to New Zealand, I started using the approach in response to reported cases of bullying.

Case study 1

A distraught fourth form (year 10) girl came to my attention as the result of a classroom discipline incident. She let it be known that she was being constantly harassed by several others in her class. The cause was a letter she was accused of writing about a relationship she had developed with a boy in the class. The victim was new to the school and was very unhappy. She denied writing the libellous letter that graphically discussed the activities of several members of the class and the boy.

In consultation with the form teacher, I called a meeting with six of her classmates, including the protagonist. At the meeting I addressed the main issue: "Rachel, a new member of the school community is very unhappy ... she feels ... " I then went on to read some of the feelings that Rachel had expressed on paper and placed the problem on the table for discussion. It was generally an unproductive discussion and the protagonist dominated the group by concentrating on what she saw as Rachel's main transgression. The others in the group were unable or unwilling to intervene.

I ended the meeting feeling unhappy and disappointed with my first attempt to use the No Blame Approach - generally feeling that perhaps New Zealand children were less susceptible to this fancy British method.

I did, however, maintain my contact with Rachel, who continued to report that she had been accepted back into the mainstream of relationships in the class. I met the group a week later and they all saw the issue as being well past them! Perhaps it did work after all.

Case study 2

Stefan, aged 13 (first year secondary - year 9) was brought to my office by a teacher after he had been found kicking the walls in a stairway. He was crying and quite agitated. Stefan had a reputation of being a professional victim with a serious temper problem. The teaching staff had little sympathy for him and believed he was the cause of a lot of his own problems.

After talking to him, it became clear that he had been persistently bullied for the last four years. He had been assaulted immediately before being found by the teacher. Once he had calmed down, I explained the No Blame Approach and asked for his permission to talk to a group of his classmates including his tormentors. He readily agreed, to my surprise, and undertook to write about his feelings that night. I also telephoned his mother and explained what I was going to do.

The next day I held a meeting to discuss the problem with a group of seven of Stefan's class (a cross-section carefully selected in consultation with the form teacher).

The subsequent discussion was absolutely fascinating. After the initial denials of any problem, the group, (beginning, I suspect, to trust the No Blame Approach), started to talk sympathetically about Stefan and the bullying problem.

While the main protagonists were flippant, the rest of the group, confronted by Stefan's piece of writing, began to sympathise with his plight. They suggested that he did not have a temper and that he put up with an enormous amount of teasing before reacting. There was a definite change in power within the group as they discussed what happened when Stefan was isolated, teased and assaulted. After about twenty minutes of discussion, I asked for ways we could solve this problem. The responses went like this:

"I could walk home with him after school."
"Stay away from him."
"Stop calling him Fuller."
"Ask him to join in with me when we do group work"
"Sit beside him."

I thanked them for their excellent and mature approach to the issue and we agreed to meet a week later to see how things were going. That meeting was brief and all agreed that they had tried to solve the problem. They said that Stefan was a much better classmate now that the bullying behaviour had stopped.

Each day for the next three weeks I made a point of seeing Stefan just to keep in touch. He assured me that things were fine. He continued to appear much happier and better behaved in class.

At the time of writing, three months after the first incident, while the physical bullying has stopped, the verbal teasing and goading have started up again. I met with the group last week and they agreed that after the holidays old habits had started up once more. The short meeting has been effective, though, as both staff and students blame Stefan for his problem, until his isolation is addressed he will continue to attract attention.

Case study 3

I became aware of Gavin's plight at a parent support evening (a monthly meeting of a group of parents) that was devoted to looking at bullying. During discussion Gavin's father started talking about Gavin's misery.

Gavin had been the victim of some particularly savage verbal rumour-mongering about his father for over a year. There was one main protagonist who had effectively alienated a whole group of Gavin's year group from him. The Dean of third form and the form teacher had, in liaison with some angry parents, taken firm action against the protagonist. They had forced public apologies and had moved the rumour-monger into a different form group. The problem had apparently gone away.

I spoke to Gavin's father, who initially was opposed to the No Blame Approach. He wanted Gavin's tormentors punished and saw the approach as being a weak response. He did, after some time, agree to let me try.

The next day I spoke with Gavin. He agreed readily to write up his feelings and was not at all resistant to the ideas of sharing these with his peers. Gavin explained that he had good friends out of his year group and had tried over the last twelve months to avoid the boys who kept making comments about his father's sexuality. He did, however, admit that he was fundamentally very unhappy, had trouble sleeping and had lost weight since the rumours had started. He observed that if anything his troubles had grown after the actions of the Dean and form teacher last year and that the group supporting his tormentor had grown.

I called a meeting of a group of six boys from Gavin's form group. We went through the steps of the approach, identifying the problems, discussing the issues and looking for solutions from within the group. Again, as in Stefan's case, I was enormously impressed by the depth of discussion and the mature approach. The boys realised the gravity of the situation and the impact their behaviour was having on Gavin. By the end of the meeting a range of solutions had been discussed and each boy had given an undertaking to work at it.

The change in Gavin was immediate. He started to look much better, the bags under his eyes went and his father was positively over the moon about the change. I see Gavin at least once a week and he has been almost totally free from any hassle since the first meeting. It all seemed so easy.

The No Blame Approach has been used on at least four other occasions in the last sixteen weeks in years 9 and 10 (Forms 3 & 4). It has been relatively successful in each case. In at least three cases the success has been outstanding, while in the other cases, the bullying has halted, albeit temporarily, and has needed further meetings as the bullying behaviour has moved targets.

The message is definitely getting through: if there is bullying, telling the teachers results in positive action. There are several important preconditions that must exist. The school needs to have a firm anti-bullying policy and needs to work hard to develop a "telling culture". The students need to have had some exposure to an anti-bullying programme, need to know what bullying is and understand relationship dynamics.

Conclusion

Colenso High School is a rich and diverse school community. We are committed to excellence in education and believe we achieve this best for all our students in a mixed ability classroom. Our student population is diverse and each class room will have the full breadth of New Zealand's economic, social and racial landscape.

Our community has few shared values and the success of the No Blame Approach in this mix is a testimony to the robust nature of the programme. If for nothing else, the experience of discussing, with a group of involved teenagers, the complex relationships that take place in adolescent groups, and being amazed at their mature, sensitive approach, is worth it.

The fact that it works so well is an added bonus.

Mark Cleary

Year Co-ordinator, Comprehensive School
Case study 1

Parents of Mandy, year 9, telephoned school to report that their daughter had returned home at lunchtime very tearful and distressed over bullying. One of her friends had recently trans-ferred to another school because of repeated intimidation. The same individual, Christine, was involved as an aggressor in both cases.

I invited Mandy and her parents into school immediately. At 4.30 pm. we discussed the situation, concentrating on Mandy and her feelings. I outlined the No Blame Approach to Mandy and her parents. At this stage they were keen to arrange a transfer for Mandy to another school, although they did comment that they were reluctant to do this because Mandy had been making good progress at Kingsfield and until recently had felt happy among her friends. Mandy and her parents agreed to give the "No Blame Approach" a try.

I asked Mandy to write a piece of prose or poetry about her feelings that I could read out at her support meeting. She did this and Mandy's brother delivered it to me the next morning.

My Feelings

"At the moment I am feeling very depressed, very lonely and think that there is really no point for me to go to Kingsfield anymore because nobody likes me. I am also very worried and frightened about walking backwards and forwards to school. If how I feel at the moment carries on, I will more than likely be moving schools. I am very tearful and feel sick and get headaches because of my fear."

In the meantime, I convened a support meeting consisting of:

- Christine - the aggressor
- Naomi - Christine's friend
- Brenda, Lucy and Mary - Mandy's friends from her tutor group who had "turned against" her.
- Mark - Mandy's friend from several of her subject lessons.
- Kirstie and Tara - Mandy's friends from year 8 who live near her.

I began the meeting by explaining the background (Mandy's feelings) and the guidelines (no punishments, no promises, no discussion of past events). I asked individuals about their feelings about the situation and whether they might find some way of helping. Mark, Kirstie and Tara were asked first. They were shocked by the degree of Mandy's distress and all offered to help in a variety of ways.

Christine and Naomi refused to help, saying "some things can't be forgiven" and "Mandy doesn't deserve help". Lucy, Brenda and Mary offered to help despite the objections that Christine and Naomi had put forward.

I thanked everyone for their time, their opinions and their suggestions and told them I would leave it up to them now. They were told that they could see me at any time and that I *would check on the situation in about a week's time.*

Christine and Naomi stayed behind at the end of the meeting. Christine wanted to know why I had never held such a meeting for her and why Mandy was getting so much attention. I explained that it was because Mandy was so very unhappy and offered to see Christine and Naomi later that day.

Mandy returned to school the following day. She walked to school with Kirstie and met up with her friends in her tutor group. She came to see me regularly during the first week after her return and reported that, although she was still frightened of Christine, she was getting help and support from her friends and other individuals, some of whom in the past associated more closely with Christine. Mandy now appears very settled. Her tutor is monitoring the situation very carefully and her friends and parents say she's much happier and beginning to enjoy school.

Christine has been involved in several incidents since the meeting. Several concerns have surfaced and Christine appears to be enduring problems which require help from an expert. She has kept in regular contact with me, as has her mother, and we have talked through problems and difficult situations. I hope that her appointment with an Educational Psychologist will help Christine to address and overcome her problems.

Case study 2.

David's poor attendance had been a cause for concern. He was sometimes described as "school phobic". His absences were always supported by letters from his parents. When he attended school, David would often report to the School Nurse feeling sick. His GP discovered that David was suffering from irritable bowel syndrome, and after seeing David, the school doctor expressed concern for David's state of health.

One morning David's mother dropped him off at school. He did not attend registration. Instead he walked to his aunt's house and spent the rest of the day there. The next day his mother bought David into school and both sat in a meeting with me.

David's mother told me that he was now refusing to come into school and that she was never sure if his illnesses were genuine. We talked matters over with David. He said that it wasn't just this school, he would feel the same about any school. Careful discussion revealed that he only ever felt really safe and happy at home. His mother supported this by saying that, al-

though he often had friends to stay overnight, David never wanted to stay overnight at their homes and had never been interested in residential school trips. David was asked about bullying but he couldn't think of anyone or anything that was upsetting him at school. Despite this, it was decided to use aspects of the No Blame Approach to help David. I called a meeting of his friends and peers, at which we discussed the situation and David's feelings. Those present were shocked by the depth and intensity of David's unhappiness and each was asked in turn to suggest a way in which they might help.

David has attended school regularly since then. Friends often call for him and accompany him to and from school. One friend in particular who has given David great support is an individual who has surprised everyone with his maturity and responsibility.

David has been referred to Child and Family guidance, although his father is not keen on this. David's case shows that aspects of the No Blame Approach can be very helpful in dealing with problems which are not related to bullying. The use of the approach seems to have helped David and also bought out very positive aspects in one of his friends who had previously been regarded as untrustworthy, irresponsible and immature.

Case study 3.

James was a very unpopular boy. He often made spiteful remarks and, sometimes, malicious attacks on other pupils. He had few friends and was frequently rude or unco-operative with subject teachers.

James came to me, complaining that he was being "picked on" by a group of boys from the same year group. I spoke to these boys and traced the antagonism back to an incident where James took one of their shoes, placed it in a lavatory bowl and pulled the flush. (This conflict began a few days before my training in the No Blame Approach).

Over the course of the next week the conflict worsened. James was pushed and tripped around school and verbally abused and chased out of school time. The group of boys would not admit to any involvement in bullying James, and James, having been a habitual liar in the past, could not be trusted to tell the whole truth.

One afternoon after school James' father telephoned me to say that he realised that his son was "no angel" but James couldn't be expected to attend school when the situation was so unpleasant. The next day I held a meeting at school with James *and his father and we decided to try the No Blame Approach. James was asked to write a piece of work about his feelings. This is what he wrote.*

"*In the morning when I'm getting ready for school I wish that I could stay at home because I know that I will get bullied during the day. When I walk to school, I can't go my usual way because I will get bullied so I have to walk across the common, which is longer than my usual way. When I get to the school gates, I have to look around the corner in case anyone is waiting to bully me.*

During registration, I am thinking about how to avoid getting bullied on my way to my first lessons. In some of my lessons I get pens, rubbers etc. thrown at me, abusive language towards me and my family, which isn't very nice and I constantly get bullied.

At break time I can't always go to the canteen because people are waiting to bully me. Sometimes I don't go to the canteen; instead I stay in school and talk to my friends. Usually when I am talking to my friends I get tripped-up, punched etc. Sometimes even chased around the school. At dinner time, I usually want to go to the ice-cream van but I can't usually get to it because people are waiting there to bully me.

Sometimes I get chased into the canteen and I can't go back out until people get fed up with chasing me. At the end of dinner time, I find it hard to get back to my tutor room because people are waiting to bully me. After registration, I have to be late for my next lesson because we line up outside the room waiting for the teacher, which means I am abused and bullied.

When the day is finished, I have to walk across the common again unless I am getting a lift which means I have to go out of the main gates. Sometimes people are waiting for me, so I can't get to my car and I have to walk home, which means that my Mum or Dad is wondering why I haven't come out of school.

This is my day at school."

The meeting was held with the four aggressors, four members of James' tutor group and a subject teacher whose presence James had specifically requested. Many feelings were discussed. The meeting agreed that James would have to make moves to help himself if others were to help him. I had already made

James and his father aware that this might be suggested. Every-one agreed that James had the right to come to school without feeling threatened. Some suggested that they could help by backing off while others offered to make more time for James provided that he treated them fairly. (One boy in particular had been treated cruelly by James in the past and was reluctant to help without this condition). Everyone was thanked for attend-ing the meeting and for their offers of help and support.

Later that day two of the aggressors came to see me. They were visibly upset and had been distressed when they realised the effect of their actions on James. They asked me if they could do more to help than just "backing off". I thanked them for coming to see me and said that perhaps we should stick to the original plan. I didn't want to create an unrealistic situation in which anyone was being artificially friendly towards James.

James, accompanied by his father, came into school the fol-lowing day. I recounted what had been said in the meeting and explained why I felt that James might return to school.

James has been back in school since then. His teacher reports that he is less isolated within his tutor group and that he is less selfish in his general behaviour towards those who are support-ing him. He has been involved in a few incidents with younger children but these have been less serious and less frequent than before. I have discussed these incidents with James and he has been able to relate the feelings of his victims to his own when he was in the same situation. The last round of assessments were James' best for over two years.

Postscript

At the start of the training (just one afternoon), I was not convinced that the No Blame Approach would be effective or that it would be appropriate in our school. I was wrong.

The best way forward for someone who is unconvinced, as I was, is to give it a go. If they really give it a fair chance and carefully follow the steps outlined, they will find out for them-selves.

For my part, I feel much more positive about my role as a Year Co-ordinator and the role of our year team. Whereas I used to feel as though I spent a good portion of my time chasing my tail, punishing and making little progress, I now feel that I am resolv-ing problems effectively. The evidence is in some of the faces of the pupils I see at school every day.

Mike Kendrick, Co-ordinator - Year 9.

The experience of a class teacher

"A" has been the victim of bullies several times before, but, for her, this occasion was the hardest to bear. Her religion set her apart from all her peers and this led to her estrangement from them in the classroom and in the playground.

She complained of name-calling, of peers refusing to work with her and of problems in the playground and out of school. Many attempts had been made to deal with the situation along conventional lines, but A's mother came into school saying the situation had gone from bad to worse. A was refusing to come to school, was constantly depressed and physically sick.

I spoke to A the following morning. She described her feelings and recorded them in a poem. She told me the names of the "bullies" and the names of the friends who she felt might support her. I met with the group and described A's feelings to them and read her poem. They suggested ways in which they might offer her support and we agreed to meet a week later.

During the next few weeks I met many times with A and her group of friends, and the "bullies" and colluders. They came to me to describe their feelings and worries, each asking for support as we worked our way through the problems - not only their concern for A, but also the commitment being asked of each of them, their relationship within the group and the difficulties experienced in returning to a natural and fluid interaction. But whenever I met the victim, "bullies" or colluders they always met me with a smile, in an easy and constructive atmosphere. There was a mutually warm feeling, which saw us through our discussions. The recollection of this "warm glow" stays with me still.

The end of term saw my departure from the school to take up another post. Before I left, I found two notes on my desk, one from A and one from one of the "bullies", each thanking me for seeing them through a difficult time.

Hilary M Leavens

An Initial Approach to Bullying.

This is a slightly longer account but we use it to demonstrate that many teachers' responses to bullying are often based on well meaning but perhaps misplaced intentions. It is often hard not to want to punish the bully.

The outline of one teacher's initial punitive responses and the movement towards a more problem-solving approach provides an account that may be relevant for many teachers.

As any teacher knows, when you get your first job in the profession, your whole concentration has to be on your classroom management. You have to learn how to deal with the attempts of the pupils to bully you. This is a favourite pastime for many pupils. It is a time to be developing anti-bullying strategies for oneself, not for the children. However, if I came across blatant bullying, my response was to bully the bully.

Looking back, I guess that I took some personal revenge, too. I certainly let the bullying child know of my displeasure, and a punishment always followed. I rarely thought to follow up: learning to be a good teacher is an exacting and time-consuming process, which takes up an inordinate amount of energy. Still, I had set the pattern. The victim wants revenge on the bully: I would be the avenger - when I came across it.

A More Structured Approach.

I teach in a secondary multicultural school in Walthamstow, London. I joined the school eight years ago after Borough reorganisation. In all the schools that I have taught in, I have tried to apply positive caring principles. Experience has taught me that caring principles need a pro-active management strategy. Paper policies are useless without effective structures, properly monitored.

My personal interest in dealing with bullying was as strong as ever. After being in the school a few years, and constantly pestering the Headteacher for a wider pastoral role in the school, I came across an advert for a Kidscape conference on bullying. "Aha!", I thought, and the head agreed to my going. I came back from the conference much enthused and told him that we were going to deal with bullying in the school. We were going to have Bully Courts. He agreed to let me have a go, probably thinking I would now stop pestering him. Little did he know!

The Action Plan.

Impatient to get on, I wanted to develop an action plan which would be practical. I sat round the kitchen table at home with my wife, Sharon, who is a social worker specialising in child protection and residential work. Another social worker, Melanie, also made an important contribution that night.

We hammered out practical approaches to the issues we had identified through brainstorming. Based on the issues, I then wrote out a list of Aims and Objectives. These were, and remain:

Aims.
(a). to provide INSET for all staff;

(b). to gain the support of staff, pupils, governors and parents through open debate and consultation, for the developing whole school strategy;

(c). to transmit the INSET into good practice;

(d). to set up institutional procedures after drawing up commonly agreed definitions of bullying;

(e). by using commonly agreed definitions of bullying, drawing up a graduated list of options available to the institutional procedures;

(f). to draw up a programme for training pupils and staff in the operation of the agreed procedures;

(g). to encourage all pupils to participate positively in the school community;

(h). to have included in all job descriptions, support for the whole school strategy on bullying;

(i). to devise a system of evaluation and constant review of the strategy.

Objectives:
(a). to devise and implement a whole-school strategy to approach and deal with the problem of bullying;

(b). to heighten the awareness of governors, parents, all staff (including ancillary staff), and pupils about the nature and problem of bullying and its consequences;

(c). to agree on common definitions for the term "bullying" within a framework of anti-discriminatory practice;

(d). to promote an environment of personal safety and a philosophy of caring in practice;

(e). to provide caring professional support for both victim and bully;

(f). to empower the victims of bullying through designated institutional procedures;

(g). to empower the onlooker.

I then took this list to the Head, who approved it.

Priorities
Our action plan called for practical strategies and recognised two initial priorities. We needed to raise awareness amongst the staff of the fact that bullying was occurring, and that we did not need to feel helpless before it either as a staff, or as individuals. The second priority was to discover the actual level of bullying taking place. Since it was already some way through the Summer

Term, I concentrated on raising the level of staff consciousness.

I invited in Francis Gobi of the Neti-Neti Theatre Company. He initially worked with a small group of pupils and teachers. The intention was to make a video that explored the bully - victim - teacher relationship. This was then presented to the whole staff, and discussion took place. As an awareness-raising session, it worked. There was not much else I could do that term, but a small platform had been erected.

I spent much of the summer holiday reading the literature. It came across very strongly that the best way to protect the victims of bullying was to ensure the punishment of the bully. If bullies refused to control their aggressive intentions, then the bottom line must be exclusion - permanent if necessary. This felt right and proper to me, though I also wanted to find a way to help the bully through counselling. However, this was a secondary concern: first, victims must be protected (as I had not been when I was a pupil at school).

After the summer, we had a training day. I had invited into school representatives of external agencies to discuss the possibility of setting up a community-based anti-bullying group. Knowing that the problems of victims can be quite deep-rooted and often have causes outside the remit of school pastoral work, I wanted to have professional expertise available and contributing to the formation of strategies. Eventually, non-teaching staff, pupils and parents would be represented at meetings.

On to the pupils

I felt ready now to begin the raising of awareness of the pupils. We planned a series of assemblies to coincide with input into the Personal and Social Education programme. It was all to culminate in a series of questionnaires to all pupils, non-teaching and teaching staff and a letter home to parents informing them what we were doing.

The questionnaires met three needs:
- *raising awareness;*
- *gathering information from everyone in the school;*
- *allowing opinions to be expressed, and solutions to be offered.*

In the meantime, an unforeseen problem arose (one of many to be experienced!). I became besieged by pupils who wanted help with a bullying problem. I also had a number of parents phoning to make appointments with me. Suddenly, time-man-

agement became a serious problem for me working, as I do, off a full timetable with other duties.

Schools wishing to deal properly with bullying and related issues, must make time for someone to do it. This has budget implications.

I had raised awareness, and now I faced demands for action and support. So I developed, overnight, a strategy based on different levels of response. These levels, enshrining a punitive response, became the bedrock of the anti-bullying policy in the school. They gave me the space I needed to take on the bullying behaviours exhibited by several of our pupils. They remained as the school policy and practice until a certain conference on No Blame in Manchester, September 1993.

The Five Levels of Response to Bullying

After running a pilot scheme for a while, the following was given out to all teachers in the school, and described in a letter to parents. We also had a special assembly where the system was explained to the pupils. When I first devised the system, I tried to include the sentiments expressed in the questionnaire replies, but, after much discussion, decided against bully courts.

Level One.

When a pupil puts a complaint into the Bully Box, the complaint is investigated. If we are reasonably certain that bullying or aggressive behaviour has taken place, the form tutor and I see those involved, and talk to them about the nastiness of bullying. It is important for the form tutor to lead in the pastoral work vital to this process.

I have found that most casual bullies will admit to what they have done when faced with the evidence. If the incident is not too serious, I ask the bully to write a letter of apology to their victim, which must be signed by their parents. At this point, I warn the disclosed bully that a repeat of the bullying/aggressive behaviour will lead to ...

Level Two.

A letter is sent home to parents informing them of the incident. At this point parents or guardians of the bully are invited into school to discuss the matter further if they wish to do so. In this letter, the parents or guardians are also informed that a further incident of bullying or aggressive behaviour will result in a temporary suspension. I have found that most parents do come *into school on receipt of this letter.*

Level Three.

Pupils who continue to bully or behave aggressively will be suspended informally (i.e. off the record). Parents will be asked into school with their child, for a consultation with the Head of Year and a Deputy Head. As with all levels, the pupil, and parents if necessary, will be offered counselling. We have found that parents often show strain when their child is discovered to be a bully. Parents will also sometimes disclose problems at home, and strains in their relationship.

Level Four.

Further bullying or aggressive behaviour will lead to a formal suspension. After a short period, the parents will be invited into school with their child for a consultation with the Deputy Head and the Headteacher. At this point, the pupil will be told that any further incidence of bullying or aggressive behaviour will result in permanent exclusion from the school. Different strategies will be used to try to ensure that the last level is not reached. These can include compulsory counselling and perhaps a contract.

Level Five.

Any further evidence of bullying or aggressive behaviour will result in permanent exclusion from the school.

The use of these levels of response was agreed by the Head and Governors of the school.

I also described in the same information pack, strategies for helping the victims of bullying. These included counselling and assertiveness training, perhaps through drama therapy. I also suggested that thoughtful and sensitive pupils could be used to befriend the victim of bullying.

Evaluation of the Strategies

I would love to be able to report that these strategies worked 100%, but this was not the case. There are a number of reasons for this, but I will concentrate on the main issue.

Victims, especially long-term, are frightened children. My objective had been to provide a system that such victims would be prepared to use, and that I would have used if such strategies had been in place when I was bullied in school.

The greatest fear of the victim is telling on the bullies. It might be possible to give protection on site, but not on the way to or from school. My bullies scored every time by telling me they would beat me up after school. This was a clear signal for me to leave at lunchtime, and not come back for some days or until my parents discovered me at home.

I had thought to combat this fear through a confidential "bully-box" system. I thought that I was succeeding, too. I was dealing with a lot of complaints of bullying. Most were what we adults would call minor: casual aggression or petty threats. I could usually deal with these by having informal chats with the pupil involved. At such a meeting, I warned them that bullying would not be tolerated in the school, and that repetition would result in punishment. I always spoke quietly at these meetings, and in a friendly fashion.

Frequently, that was enough. In return, I developed an increased reputation as someone not to cross.

We did work on the "conspiracy of silence" and the role of bystanders. I wanted to generate an atmosphere where bullying would have no place. Though I am aware that this is an ideal, a lot of work can be done to achieve it. It depends on how self-aware a school community is prepared to be, and how prepared they are to act on what they find.

Nevertheless, despite the effort made, bullying was still happening in school. I had dealt with a number of identified bullies, and with some success. However, I had only managed to give confidence to some of the longer-term victims. Only a few had come forward, though some were identified by other pupils or by their parents. I was beginning to feel that I would not have used the system if I was the bullied pupil.

To check the feedback I was getting, I organised another questionnaire. This was again backed up with curriculum work directed towards all year groups, as was the questionnaire. The objective was to maintain the raised awareness and find out if the levels of response were working.

The questionnaire, which was very extensive, showed a heightened sense of awareness, but it also showed that both the bully boxes and the levels of response had weaknesses. Some pupils were being threatened that if they put a note into the box, it would be found out and they would be beaten up. It was also reported that pupils were told that the boxes were watched, and that anyone putting a note in was known (this was not true). Fear still ruled response. Some pupils complained that they had put a note in, and nothing had happened. This˄ showed up the time-management problems that I constantly signalled up to anyone who would listen.

There were three major failings of the levels of response indicated by the questionnaire results. They did not help the child who bullies, but rather, as a punishment-based strategy, ensured pressure on the bully. For some pupils, this was indeed a threat that made them stop, but without tackling the causes of their exhibiting bullying behaviour.

Secondly, the heavy response to the evidence of bullying, that I always ensured, drove longer-term bullies (as opposed to casual one-off offenders) to threaten their victims even more than they already did. They went round all their victims ensuring a beating up if their name appeared in the bully boxes.

Thirdly, the system depended on my energy. All cases of bullying were being referred to me, making even bigger inroads into the amount of time available. If I left the school though, the anti-bullying work would leave with me. There was nobody to take over from me. I was identified as "Mr. Bully".

All of this disturbed me a great deal, but I had nothing to put in place of the levels of response strategy. "Anyway", I reasoned, "at least we are attempting to deal with bullying, and that is better than nothing". I still agree with that sentiment, but at the time I found it quite depressing. I recognised that I would not have used the system if I was a pupil in the school. I had not met the criteria my child-self demanded.

No Blame: Enter the Cavalry.

I would like to report that I began a systematic search for a better strategy, but this is not the case. I knew that most of the criticisms of the levels of response, though accurate, could be remedied by my being given an appropriate amount of time.

I argued, both in writing, and in discussion with the Governors and the Head, for a substantive post. By this time, though, we were operating most of our own budget, and money was very tight. I argued, therefore, knowing that what I was asking for was not possible. Because I was now giving training and advice to other schools, I thought the Borough might be interested. We had a series of meetings with the Director of Education, but no finance was forthcoming, only encouragement.

So I wasn't really looking for something to replace my system, but rather the time to make it work properly. What propelled me to look elsewhere was an Ofsted report, which criticised what I was doing for being outmoded. Had I thought to apply the No Blame Approach?

My first question, never answered despite several attempts to raise it, was in what way could any attempt to deal with bullying be considered "outmoded", when many schools have no active policy?

My second question was, "What the hell is No Blame?"

My third question was, "How can you not blame someone when bullying is taking place?"

The summer holiday intervened, and I could find no more information on No Blame. Essentially, I forgot about it until I saw a conference announced on the subject to be held in Manchester.

Maines and Robinson

I went to the conference to argue. A bottom line for me has always been protection for the victim of bullying. If you do not identify who the bully is, and prevent a repetition of the behaviour, in what way are you providing protection? If you are not seen to be punishing bullying, why should any victim risk coming forward? I wanted my questions answered!

As a perpetual student, I am aware that the best approach to being critical of any concept is first to understand it. To understand something, first there must be listening without prejudice. So despite my reservations, I was prepared to listen before passing comment. Nice of me really!

My clearest memory is when I first began to take what was being said seriously. This was when, early on in the proceedings, George and Barbara described the various responses of pupils accused of being bullied, and the various responses from teachers doing the accusing. I recognised so many of the situations and emotions described.

I recognised, for instance, the immediate confrontation caused between the teacher and the accused. I acknowledged the difficulty of proving bullying in the face of constant denial. I had always reasoned in such situations that the knowledge that I was making enquiries would make an actual bully lie low, and show that I was being active. Pupils did not want me to accuse them of bullying. (I had certainly got the heightened awareness I was constantly after!) However, the questionnaire results showed me that I was sometimes making things worse for the victim: an intolerable situation. Perhaps in the end, that is why I was so receptive to No Blame.

The point that George and Barbara were trying to sensitise the conference to, was that punishment-based strategies of response, like mine, were counterproductive. In such systems, might is shown to be right, even though we punish the bully for applying that principle. We then label both bully and victim, and treat them accordingly. We easily become blind to the other behaviours, strengths, weaknesses and personal history that make up the whole of a person, whether bully, victim, colluder or bystander. This implies that our help is superficial at best, though well-intended.

In the afternoon session, we were shown the No Blame process. The key to No Blame is that it is an exercise in empathy-building. It seemed to me to be an exciting extension of the work I was doing on changing the atmosphere of the school, and the emphasis I was putting on "no bystanders": everyone has responsibility for everyone else; be sensitive to the needs of others as well as your own needs; pupils have the right to not be bullied, you do not have the right to stay silent about it. Most importantly, No Blame was suggesting a way to help both victims and bullies by using, and therefore giving responsibility to, colluders and bystanders.

The No Blame Approach seemed to offer a radical structure to help achieve the aims and objectives I had started out with.

Back to School.

The proof of the pudding is in the eating. I returned to school, discussed the implications of the No Blame Approach with my Head and the anti-bully group, and then began to wait for a suitable candidate. One was not long in coming.

Tom was a year 7 pupil. He found things quite tough when he first entered the school. His form tutor, a very experienced teacher, signalled up to me that Tom seemed to have no friends, and was being bullied by other members of his class. Time to use No Blame.

I set up the support group exactly as suggested in the No Blame steps provided in the literature. Assuring Tom that I was not going to be punishing anybody, and therefore giving no-one a reason to seek revenge, encouraged him to be very forthcoming. After an initial hesitation he became quite fluid in his speech. Just the telling was an emotional release for him.

Tom chose his group members and I arranged for the form tutor to bring the group together. They were all very nervous about meeting with us. We put them at their ease as much as possible, by assuring them they were not in any kind of trouble; in fact we wanted their help and they had been chosen because we thought they could handle it.

I read out what Tom had agreed to, and then asked how they thought we could all help: how we could enhance Tom's quality of life in school. They were silent for a little while, and then the suggestions began to come out. They were simple things such as:

"I'll give him sweets."

"I'll get him to come and play football with us."

"I'll sit next to him in lessons and work with him in a group."

The most telling response came from the boy who bullied him the most. He told us that he would become Tom's friend.

We thanked the group for their help, and left them to it. I left it a few days before I could no longer resist checking on Tom. He was bright and cheerful. He said he was much happier. Some of the group had told others in the class to leave him alone, and he wasn't being bothered by anyone.

The next time I saw Tom, he had a friend with him. This boy was the one who said he would become Tom's friend. They have been inseparable since.

The success of this group encouraged me to try another group. This was with a year 8 pupil. Again I went through the No Blame process. The form tutor involved relaxed the chosen group by providing biscuits and Coke: an excellent idea. This group again proved successful, with the pupil concerned in school with friends, where before he had been finding it difficult to make any.

Nobody got punished, yet the bullying stopped and the victims settled into the school. A very encouraging start.

As other victims came to our notice, probably because of an awareness maintaining campaign at the beginning of the academic year, we continued to use No Blame as a first level of response. I kept in place the levels of response described earlier as a back-up if a group failed to prevent bullying. The bottom line will always remain protection of the victim.

Extending the No Blame Approach.
Pupil Support Groups.

No Blame is not simply a method for dealing with bullying. At its heart is a non-punitive philosophy which, if properly utilised, has an impact on all aspects of pastoral management strategies. Bearing this in mind, what I have found to be a most appealing aspect of No Blame is the strategy of helping children to help each other.

Why limit this co-operation to bullying? Some pupils come into school with heavy baggage: others need help because of an event in their home lives such as a bereavement. Whatever the circumstances, those best placed to offer support are other children.

Case Studies.
Paul

Paul, at age 13, was a new entrant to the school. It was his third secondary school. Immediately after joining us, Paul's mother came to school to complain that he was being bullied. I interviewed both of them together. Paul was quite quiet: his mother told me the story. We have in year 9, a pupil who was in conflict with Paul when they were at primary school. Then it had been Paul who was doing the bullying. Paul was saying that the boot was on the other foot now.

I admit to having my doubts about what I was being told. However, I promised to look into it. I also spoke about the support group that we could offer.

After further investigation and consultation with the Head of Year, we decided a support group would be a useful induction for Paul. We put him in a class where we thought the boys could be of help. I chose the group members because Paul did not know anybody. I explained to the boys what was required. Those who have been involved in the support groups had no problem with the role I requested of them.

Our ultimate intention with Paul was to ensure his continued attendance at school. We wanted to provide him with friends so that he had a good reason for coming to school. His behaviour in his other schools had been such that they felt they could not contain him.

I also chose two of the naughtier boys in the class. I suspected that Paul would gravitate to them anyway, and I wanted to see if they could respond to the role I was giving them without leading him into trouble. This caused some surprise to the Head of Year and Form tutor, but we had to try this as well: support groups are intended to be supportive of all involved. We determined to keep an active eye on Paul's situation and settling-in process.

The bullying stopped immediately. This was not so much the support group, but rather that I had seen the other boy involved, who was not known as an aggressive child. He admitted that he had been seeking revenge for earlier problems, but said that he would not continue to do so if he was left alone. I trusted him, and this turned out to be justified.

Paul did indeed become close friends with one of the naughtier boys in the support group. They helped each other keep out of trouble, and Paul became a regular attender at school. He also began to show that he had some abilities other than winding-up teachers.

It is important to note that this support group needed close support from the form tutor in the early stages. The main emphasis was for the boys to be nice to Paul. We had been stressing this message for quite some time, in both curriculum and anti-bullying terms, so the boys knew what they had volunteered for.

Our discussions with the group were about heightening their awareness, and discussing things that could happen to Paul in the normal course of the day and ways to deal with them. This included conflicts with teachers. We suggested that Paul could be brought out of the class he was in to any of us if things were getting a bit conflictual with pupils or teacher. We also informed all teachers that this was part of the general support system.

One year later, Paul continues to attend school (on a fairly regular basis!), and is not (often!) found in trouble. We removed the support group structure as soon as we judged that it had met its objectives. Paul became a fairly popular member of the form group. His reputation was enhanced when he, and a (naughty) member of the support group, appeared on national radio to talk about how the support group had helped him. It was good feedback.

Ravinder

Ravinder was 12 when I was asked to help with him. He was a truant who had missed many months of schooling. The Education Welfare Officer had made a number of visits to his home but, even with parental support, she had not managed to get Ravinder to attend school.

Obviously, our thoughts turned to bullying. With the Head of Year's agreement, I made a home visit. After an initial hesitation, he told me he was not being bullied, but he had found it difficult to make any friends. He told me this with great embarrassment.

Ravinder had acknowledged that he did like some of the other pupils. This gave me my way in. I left him to write down, just for himself, his feelings. Meantime I went back to school to see the two boys he had mentioned. They were sensible lads, and willing to help. We talked for a while about Ravinder, and then, with their agreement, arranged for them to make a visit to Ravinder that afternoon.

This first visit, where they just chatted and played computer games, was a great success. Two days later, after a second evening visit, Ravinder came into school. The two boys continued to support him, just by including him in what they were doing. We made sure that Ravinder was put into the same teaching groups as them. This was always... intended as a small support group which, though not wholly successful in that he was not there every day, certainly helped lighten the load for Ravinder.

After the encouraging performance of these pilot groups of children learning to help each other, with the active support of the form tutor or Head of Year, we decided, as we had with bullying, to make the Pupil Support Groups a first level of response to the whole range of disruptive problems that children experience as a barrier to learning.

There are mixed results to report. This strategy has helped some, but not others. It is quite possible that by the time some pupils reach the age to come to us, they are already alienated beyond our approaches and skills. Such a pupil was Wesley.

Wesley

Wesley, aged 12, exhibited both bullying behaviour and classroom disruption. The school was close to permanently excluding him. We decided to try a support group around him. When I talked to him about the support group idea, he seemed to like it. In preparation, I asked him to write a little bit about himself. In the process, I was hoping to help him understand himself a bit better. The plan was for Wesley to help choose the members of his support group, and reveal something of himself to them. With his form tutor's help, I gathered the group, some of whom I had chosen and which included Year 10 pupils.

We spoke to the group about Wesley. The pupil at the centre of the group should not usually attend the meetings. In bullying cases, it would be too much of a strain for the victims; in general cases, it would not allow free discussion of strategies.

Essentially, however, the group was formed too late. Wesley

had already become too alienated from the school, and pupils in it. He had devised a simple plan to get himself thrown out of school. Pastoral staff had put in a large amount of work on him for what appeared to be little return. Before the support group could really get to work, Wesley blew his top at a teacher.

I spoke to Wesley before he left. He wanted to show to me the writing that he had done about himself. It was really very thoughtful. I feel that if we had had a support group system embedded into pastoral management, we could have helped Wesley to come to terms with his temper and aggressive behaviour. He had certainly liked the idea, but gave it no time to work.

From these and other support groups in the areas of under achievement and classroom disruption, many lessons were learned. Not all the groups were successful, but each No Blame or Pupil Support Group gave insights into how pupils can be better supported by the use of the strategy. They encouraged a de-labelling process for both pupils and staff because of the strong presence of the pupil at the centre of the group. They provided a proactive support structure, which heightened the sense of responsibility, and enhanced the maturity, of the pupils who formed the support. This in turn had an impact on the general atmosphere of the school, which was noted by both staff and pupils.

Non-Teaching Staff and No Blame Support Groups.

The school is a community with a strict division of labour. This is strongly indicated by having staff meetings for teachers only. In doing so, we ignore the experiences and talents of a number of adults in the school.

Recognising this, the anti-bully group in school had representatives from the non-teaching staff. In order to include this category of staff in the anti-bullying work, they were asked to complete a questionnaire about their perceptions of school life. I wanted to raise their awareness as an equally important part of the school community. I also wanted to know what they had seen, since they see parts others do not see, and ask for suggestions on ways to combat bullying.

The information given back did indeed show areas of weakness in the duty system. Some of the kitchen staff said they were aware of bullying, but did not feel capable of stopping it when some of the lads were so big. They occasionally felt intimidated themselves. We have tried to rectify this by changing the duty system, and I took their views into account when developing anti-bullying strategies. I had also asked if they would like training on intervention strategies, but only a few said they wanted to be so involved. I would have liked to follow this up properly, but the demon Time had too many other demands to make on me, and I wasn't sure what role they could play, except as eyes and ears - which is what happened, and very useful it is too!

However No Blame groups, and other types of support groups based on the No Blame model, are a vehicle for involving those non-teaching staff who want to have a wider role in the school community.

The Senior Technician in school, Linda, has been an active member of the anti-bullying group since it began, and a constant motivator whenever I began to feel I was banging my head against a wall because of the slow progress. So when I decided that it was time for a non-teacher to have a go, I naturally turned to Linda, who was immediately enthusiastic.

Linda was a good person to start with, for a number of reasons, the main one being that she has a lot of contact with the pupils through her role as the nominated first-aid person. Another important reason is her knowledge about, and sensitivity towards, bullies and victims. She is fully supportive of the No Blame philosophy and approach.

This is an ongoing group at the time of writing, but I would like to quote part of Linda's report. The context of the quote is the day after she had pulled the support group together to talk about the victim, Tony.

Tony

"The day after the first meeting of the group, four of the boys were with Tony at lunch-time in the playground. Tony spent a lot of the time hanging the boys' coats on a tree. One of the group passed the cricket bat to him and he briefly joined in their game. When the whistle went at the end of lunch, all the boys came back into school together.

When I saw some of the group with Tony, I felt elated: something was working. I am very hopeful that the boys will continue to help Tony. I will keep a close watch on the situation, and if need be, will call the group together again."

The next report from Linda reads:

"I saw Tony this morning and asked him how he was. He had the biggest grin on his face that I had seen for a long time. He said he was happy as the boys were now playing with him. One boy was now walking part of the way home with him, and he enjoyed the company. I am hoping that the group can keep up the momentum!"

There are complications with Tony that go beyond his being bullied, but a non-teaching member of staff is having a major, structured, impact on the life of some of the boys in school, as well as enhancing her own skills and reputation.

We are now offering training in No Blame and general support group procedures to other schools. Linda will be an important part of the work. While I talk to the teaching staff, she will be with non-teaching staff. This is part of the process of recognising the role of such staff. It always helps schools to have more eyes and ears as part of the awareness raising process, and some non-teaching staff might want to go further, as has happened in my school.

Conclusions

At the conference in Manchester, I remember asking if No Blame was being put forward as a universal panacea. Barbara had said what the high success rate was before I asked the question. After all my initial intent was to ask critical questions, but this was the only critical point I was left with.

I can now easily answer that question myself; there is no such thing, and the No Blame process is not intended to be taken in that way. What it provides is a non-punitive response to violent and aggressive behaviours. At its most superficial level, it provides the building blocks for empathy and a caring philosophy. It gives all pupils a chance, and offers all pupils structured support.

Some children will reject the help offered, as has happened in my experience, and will need other strategies. As a first level of response, however, I am very satisfied with the progress made, and, on a personal level, I no longer want to take revenge on the bullies. My experience is that punishment for the sake of revenge is frequently counterproductive.

Dave Brown.

Chapter 11

Promoting the
No Blame
Approach

We have promoted the No Blame Approach through our training video and by running workshops in places as diverse as Adelaide and Birmingham, Washington (USA) and Durham, Istanbul and Islington. Our colleagues Julian Forsey, Jane Sleigh and Jonathan Coles have presented workshops all over Britain, and many other professionals actively support the approach by using the training package. We have also received an enormous amount of encouragement from two people: Lorraine Demko, of Eastern Surrey Health Promotion Unit, and Gillian Harding, of Greater Nottingham Training and Enterprise Council. Both have established innovative, long-term projects using the No Blame Approach, and both have contributed accounts of their programmes. We acknowledge our gratitude to them both.

Eastern Surrey Health Promotion Unit

Over the past few years, bullying has become a very topical issue and one about which there has been great public concern. At times the media coverage has been intense, sensationalising the horrific and distressing circumstances in which some young people have taken their own lives.

Bullying has become a concern for educationalists and parents alike. Parents' demands to know what their children's schools are doing about bullying have often stimulated the search for more effective ways of dealing with the problem. This has enabled schools to show that they are caring and safe environments for young people to learn in.

However, many of the current policies for dealing with bullying are punitive, and deter victims from reporting incidents for fear of reprisals; such policies may also lead some bullies to take their own lives for fear of the punitive measures taken by some schools.

In Eastern Surrey Health Authority the Health Promotion Unit has been working, in alliance with the LEA, Educational Psychologists and schools from the state and independent sector, towards a whole-school approach for dealing with bullying. The No Blame Approach has been adopted as an effective response which can be used together with more general work on awareness and prevention. This creates an approach that brings the whole school community together to develop an effective anti-bullying policy.

In 1993, a pilot project in one school developed a model of good practice using the No Blame Approach. The model is now used to help other schools to plan, develop and implement their own approaches, thus enabling them to create safer schools. The programme has gone through several phases, from raising awareness of the issues around bullying to implementing a whole-school approach. Each of the schools involved has been given advice, support, and training in the No Blame Approach, together with the resources needed to develop effective interventions. Sharing good practice with other schools has provided opportunities for schools to network with each other, while respecting the individuality of each school and the different needs that have to be addressed throughout the process.

Eastern Surrey Health Promotion Unit believes that every young person has the right to reach his or her personal and academic potential and should be safe and secure in school. Sadly, this is not the case for many young people, who suffer the humiliation and pain of being bullied for long periods in their schooling. The effects, however, do not end there, because persistent bullying erodes the self-confidence and self-esteem of victims to such an extent that their social interactions may remain affected as adults. Research also suggests that bullying has a damaging influence on the whole atmosphere of a school, affecting not only the victims, but also those who passively witness the attacks or threats, who can become both anxious and distressed.

Eastern Surrey Health Promotion Unit is currently funding this health promotion programme. Funding was previously provided by the Department of Public Health and then by the Health Authority. The programme has been identified as a priority for Eastern Surrey, and will continue to be supported by the health promotion unit.

Two quotations from local schools show what they feel the No Blame Approach has given them:

> "Development through the curriculum, and a whole-school approach to anti-bullying behaviour, have greatly enhanced awareness among pupils, staff and parents. The response and empathy that have been generated through our policy have led to a successful implementation of the No Blame Approach."
> **Head of Senior School, Ewell Castle School, May 1995.**

> "... because of our school's approach to discipline and the care of children, the ideas behind the 'No Blame Approach' were compatible with the school ethos. We

have found, since using this approach, that the children are more helpful and responsive with information and solutions. There is much more openness in communication, and teachers are more aware of their role in dealing with bullying behaviour."

Head, Kingswood House School, September 1996

Lorraine Demko

Greater Nottingham Training and Enterprise Council
Coping with Challenging Behaviour - a TEC's response

In the summer of 1995, a series of articles in local and national newspapers highlighted the plight of school children who suffered both mentally and physically at the hands of bullies, and were, in some cases, driven to the point of total despair and attempted suicide. At the same time a report - Bullying in Two Nottingham Comprehensives - by Community Paediatrician Dr. Vidya Rao, of Nottingham University, found that:

- *one in three children were likely to be abused at least once a term*
- *one in eight children were frequently bullied*
- *one in five were called nasty names*
- *almost one in ten were hit and kicked*
- *almost one in five admitted taking part in bullying staff*
- *one in four admitted to being frequent bullies while only one in five said they would never menace others.*

Child health workers now accept that one child suicide in ten is related to bullying.

Media attention also began to focus on workplace bullying, with alarming statistics being quoted about the cost to British industry of the loss of production, absenteeism and ill health as a result of employees suffering bullying at work. The late Andrea Adams campaigned for recognition of workplace bullying and for it to be addressed separately, with clear guidance for companies on how to recognise and handle situations. Bullying was generally dealt with as a form of harassment, but, unlike sexual or racist harassment, there were no clear directives on how to approach the taboo subject.

In her keynote speech at an MSF Union Conference on bully-

ing, Andrea Adams said: "In Britain, this problem continues to be swept under the carpet, largely because of its association with the school playground. It is clearly too embarrassing for many organisations to openly acknowledge that this could be happening in their particular workplace. There is actually an important link between school bullying and workplace bullying. Just like the child, terrified of going to school to be taunted all over again, adults being bullied in the workplace are reduced to the state of frightened children. As one man described it to me, "It made me feel as if I were five again". No wonder people have described this experience of going to the office as like entering the cage of an unpredictable animal, to face another week of professional crucifixion.

So why does it so often go undetected? The fact is that complaints about such ill-treatment are typically dismissed as a personality clash or bad attitude, or strong, robust management, or working in a funny way. Call it bullying and the organisation is more than likely to throw up its hands in horror. Bullying is always somebody else's problem and never theirs. Things like that happen in school playgrounds and not, apparently, in respectable places of work. Yet, name-calling is just as prevalent in the workplace as it is in the school playground."

Few articles offered anything other than a sensational story, with little or no information on practical ways of coping or dealing effectively with bullying. However, the 30 June 1995 edition of the Times Educational Supplement printed a selection of case studies, editorials and responses to bullying. Amongst these was "Why The No Blame Approach Can Work For Adults Too". The piece described the No Blame Approach as a proven strategy that worked for both children and adults, whether at school or in the workplace. Teaching unions had also expressed an interest in the approach, not for use with children, but for workplace bullying. It was this article which led to GNTEC's partnership with George Robinson and Barbara Maines, and the development of a training programme for both businesses and schools offering preventive and reactive strategies for bullying through the No Blame Approach.

"Creating prosperity by investing in people" is GNTEC's mission statement. Embodied in this is the philosophy that all individuals have the opportunity to fulfil their potential. The economic wealth and prosperity of a region are dependent upon its people and their achievements. But what of the barriers to potential and the cost of under-achievement and failing performance? What active role can a TEC play in seeking to address these issues and helping to break down some of the hidden barriers? It was the Education Business Partnership that provided the platform to address the issues of both workplace and school bullying.

The training programme began in November 1995 with a one-day conference: "Coping with Challenging Behaviour in both the Workplace and School". Led by George and Barbara, 25 schools and 25 companies examined the problem of bullying, sharing experiences and knowledge, identifying characteristics of bullying behaviour and challenging traditional responses to bullying incidents. The process allowed them to consider and assess the No Blame Approach and whether or not it was a feasible strategy to adopt within their respective establishments. As a follow-up to the day, the teachers paired off with a company and visited the premises to examine in more depth corporate strategies (where they existed) for dealing with workplace bullying.

In preparing for the conference, it became apparent that little written information or advice was readily available to companies. Sweden is currently the only country offering clear legislation and specific guidance to business on victimisation at work. The Swedish Embassy forwarded copies of the booklet Victimisation at Work (AFS 1993:17) for issue to delegates.

The conference was successful in raising awareness of bullying and its consequences. Fifteen of the schools asked to receive follow-up visits from George or Barbara to talk with the senior management teams on how the No Blame Approach could be used in their particular school. Company personnel also felt that the day had been useful in challenging assumptions on what bullying at work was, and they valued the opportunity to reflect on their corporate approach to the problem. They were not, however, so responsive to the idea of follow-up visits, but preferred to take away the supporting literature for consideration.

Whilst the programme still offered joint training opportunities on the No Blame Approach for schools and companies, the focus would need to be split between child and adult bullying. Teachers could readily see applications in the approach for dealing with pupils, but agreed with business that, as regards bullying in the staff room or work place, a separate programme was required on the No Blame Approach for Adults. The focus for the following year, 1996, therefore became child bullying, whilst research and preparation continued for the adult programme.

The year began by supporting Haywood School, Nottingham with a Whole School Awareness Day on bullying in January. The day was planned with the help of George Robinson and resulted in normal lessons being suspended so that staff and pupils (aged from 11 to 16) could work together during the day. A group of actors and musicians from the Armadillo Theatre Company ran drama and music workshops, helping staff and pupils to explore what is meant by bullying and how people are affected. The children also wrote and performed poems and plays, painted pictures and worked in a practical way to consider where bullying takes place within the school, highlighting danger zones and identifying what could be done to stop bullying. Participants also included parents and teachers from the family primary schools. The day was very successful and also gained a lot of positive media coverage for the school and the No Blame Approach, with both BBC and Central TV present, the Nottingham Evening Post represented and radio interviews broadcast on BBC Radio Nottingham, Radio Trent and Radio 5 Live.

The day also marked the beginning of an extra dimension to the programme with the use of interactive drama as a powerful training tool. The 1996-7 schools' programme - "Coping with Challenging Behaviour" - was developed jointly between GNTEC, George and Barbara, and Armadillo Theatre. The pilot programme aimed to:

- raise the awareness of each school community about bullying and its consequences
- educate all school staff and students in the No Blame Approach to bullying
- train all school staff in both preventive and reactive measures to reduce bullying within their community
- work with Year 7 pupils through a PSE programme
- work with a group of Year 10 students on developing and delivering a drama workshop for Year 6 pupils in their feeder primary schools in order to improve links between the schools
- bring together the activity into a whole-school policy on bullying and monitor the impact of the programme within each school.

Schools which attended the November 1995 conference were invited to take part in the one year programme (see p. 138), and six chose to do so. The programme sought to combine a variety of training methods, as illustrated particularly well by the INSET day, with its use of interactive drama rather than video footage to bring to life the pain and impact of bullying on people's lives. The technique also proved to be a powerful teaching aid in showing people how to use the No Blame techniques when dealing with a bullying case. The formula of combining the joint talents of George and Barbara with those of Armadillo Theatre proved an effective one, with the INSET day rated overall as excellent by 82% of all participants:

"this has been the best training day I have had in my seven years of teaching. For the first time I have learnt something."

"useful to challenge current practices and beliefs."

"the drama was very useful in understanding the victim's point of view."

"the drama was a most useful enactment of the No Blame Approach."

"an alternative approach offered with evidence of success."

"I thoroughly enjoyed the day - the best ever INSET!"

"I would love George and Barbara to come back again to do further work. Their presentation skills are excellent, very professional."

"school needs to consider fully how this fits in with other approaches."

"the INSET was certainly not specific to a secondary age group - as a junior school teacher, thank you."

"excellent - best INSET I have had - thought-provoking. All schools should have this training even if they choose not to adopt the approach."

The 1996-97 'Coping with Challenging Behaviour' Programme involved:

- INSET Days - 5 Schools: 225 adults (teaching/non teaching)
- Whole School Awareness Days - 6 Schools: 3015 students
- Year 7 PSE - 5 schools: 525 students
- Year 10 Drama - 5 Schools: 20 students

- Feeder School performances - 15 Schools: 750 Year 6 pupils
- Planning and Policy Workshop - 6 Schools: 9 senior staff

The Planning and Policy Workshop in April 1997 with George and David Gilligan (of Armadillo Theatre) offered each school an opportunity to describe its individual programme and the subsequent action taken, and to discuss these with other schools. Time was also allocated in the day to agree with the trainers and the TEC how the programme could be developed further in each school, and what continued support was needed.

1997/98 sees the schools coming full circle in terms of George and Barbara's work. Their approach to bullying, and the development of the No Blame Approach, were born out of their self-concept work. Through the 'Coping with Challenging Behaviour' programme, the six pilot schools have opened their doors to a wider discussion on the issues of behaviour management and the revision of their behaviour policies. In seeking to help all children fulfil their potential and to remove barriers to their success, the schools are now considering self-concept as an influence on successful learning, examining strategies for making punishment positive and using ways of speaking to children which communicate important feelings. Bullying will be discussed as a particular illustration of the ineffectiveness of punishment.

In addition to the schools exploring these self-concept theories, they will continue with Armadillo Theatre and an anti-bullying maintenance programme for the students. The key to the continued impact of the anti-bullying approach is the year 7 PSE programme for each intake, and the follow-up work in year 8. The year 10 drama curriculum gives older students valuable workshop skills and enhances links with the primary schools, while spreading a coherent approach to dealing with bullying amongst families of schools.

The GNTEC Workplace Bullying Programme is still under development. Since 1995, progress has been made, with many of the unions revising policies and guidelines for member companies and gaining parliamentary support for legislation. The Dignity at Work Bill failed to pass through the House of Lords, its fate sealed by the timing of the General Election, but it did attempt to give recognition to what constitutes workplace bullying.

Workplace bullying has always occurred. It is unacceptable,

disruptive and extremely costly. The Industrial Society publication, Briefing Plus (June 1997), reported research undertaken by Professor Cary Cooper, at the University of Manchester Institute of Science and Technology, which indicated that bullying can be the reason for nearly half of all the stress-related illness which affects employees. Given that the Health and Safety Executive calculates that 80 million working days are lost in the UK each year through mental health problems (at a cost of between £6 and £7 billion), employers should be aware that bullying may be costly in terms of absence, high staff turnover, poor performance levels, lost business and a lack of competitiveness, all of which may result from the stress caused by bullying.

Often education has to follow the lead and use best practice from industry, but in the case of bullying, schools are showing companies the way forward, and demonstrating how to deal with bullying, to the benefit of all concerned. Education Business Partnerships are able to bring both sectors together to work on tackling a common problem with a joint approach. The common aims of the school and workplace anti-bullying programmes are to:

- *raise awareness of bullying and its consequences*
- *educate adults and young people in the No Blame Approach*
- *train adults in both preventive and reactive measures to reduce bullying*
- *help organisations and institutions to review their policies on behaviour or harassment*
- *help create a safe environment for people to learn and work in which to maximise their potential.*

Thanks and acknowledgments to:
George Robinson and Barbara Maines
Armadillo Arts
Alderman Derbyshire School
Dayncourt Comprehensive
Colonel Frank Seely School
Foxwood Special School
Haywood School
Manning School for Girls and their partner primary schools
Swedish Embassy, London
GMB Union, Nottingham
GPMU, Nottingham.

Gillian Harding

COPING WITH CHALLENGING BEHAVIOUR
SCHOOLS' PROGRAMME
April 1996 - March 1997

Briefing Session
School complete a briefing session with GNTEC to agree and sign up to one year programme.

INSET Day
<u>Whole school</u> staff day (including all non teaching staff) on The No Blame Approach to coping with challenging behaviour.

Awareness Day
Whole school awareness day raising the issue of bullying and its consequences and how to tackle it.

Year 7 PSE Workshops
Whole of year 7 receive a seven week PSE programme focusing on dealing with bullying.

Year 10 drama workshops to year 6
Two week programme for group of year 10 students to develop and deliver drama performances to year 6 pupils in feeder schools.

Teacher Placements
One five day placement completed within the time span of the programme exploring bullying in the workplace and school.

Policy Conference
One day conference for participating schools to share good practice and focus on final stage of developing and writing their school policies.

Analysis - Outcomes
Reports in from schools detailing progress of the year's programme. Video recordings presented.

School Policy
First draft of school policy to be completed. Framework for continuing work into 1997/98.

Chapter 12

Conclusion

We have not used all the contributions we received. There comes a point where extra words, though individually powerful, do not add to the message.

We have not dwelt on the variations using the same philosophy of a non-punitive, caring and problem-solving approach.

One parent wrote after Barbara had created "caring teams" round two boys locked in an interchangeable bully/victim syndrome and involved both sets of parents:

In short, Barbara carried out several sessions with the boys enrolling "team friends" to support each of them and kept us fully informed through the head teacher of progress over time. The net result, in an amazingly short time, was that the situation was not only resolved but a culture of care and concern was cultivated along the way which has spilled over into the wider class environment and not least into a mutual respect and even friendship between us and the parents of the boy concerned.

Will Grealish, parent.

A secondary head of year, who became a deputy head in the time scale of the account, wrote how her approach to pupils changed after attending a No Blame training day.

She wrote before the training:

I was Head of Keller House at Thamesmead School. The House system is a very strong pastoral structure within our school and each House Head feels a great sense of responsibility towards the pupils in his or her care. I was no exception to this. Keller students were "my" students. Perhaps this is why I reacted so bitterly when I learnt that one of them, a new Year 8 girl, was distressed because another Year 8 girl, from another House, was tormenting her.

I was furious! How dare this girl, Carol, upset one of my girls. I demanded to see Carol and heaped on her all my feelings of anger and resentment, I showed nothing but sympathy for the poor "victim" and I forced Carol into a meaningless apology, delivered in a sullen and insincere tone. She left the room burning with hatred. I don't think she was unkind to the girl again, I have to admit I never checked, but I had definitely made an enemy. Nevertheless, I felt I had dealt with the incident efficiently. As I passed Carol in the corridors, I was aware of a great hostility towards me, but apart from that there were no repercussions.

I had no more dealings with Carol until nearly two years later when, during a Health and Safety Week that I had organised, the pupils were given talks on sexual relationships and the use of contraceptives. One day the school nurse, who was delivering the talks, came to me rather dismayed to have discovered that some of the condoms she had brought in to show the pupils had gone missing. After investigating, I found out that they had been taken by Carol and another boy and handed around in the playground. When dealing with Carol on this occasion I was met with the same hostility and resentment that I had experienced before. She seemed again to be feeling that she was suffering a great injustice, even though she admitted taking the condoms. Letters were sent home and the boy's parents were very support- ive of any punishment on our part. However Carol's mother blamed the whole thing on the fact that Carol felt I had never liked her ever since I had accused her of bullying in her first year with us. She felt that I picked on her, and that I was treating the boy more leniently. (They were in fact both dealt with in the same way.) Throughout the following year, as Carol and I passed in the corridor, I was aware of her resentment towards me.

In 1992, I attended a one day course on The No Blame Ap- proach to bullying. By this time, I had already progressed from the teacher who had shouted vehemently at Carol for being unkind to one of "my" girls. I had dealt with other problems more sensitively, and this approach formalised in my mind a response to bullying that I had begun to use instinctively. It was a brilliant day.

Another incident arose with Carol. Although the teacher did not follow the normal 7 steps, she implemented the philosophy of No Blame and sought to gain the support of one of the protagonists by highlighting the victim's fears. The victim was reluctant to name anybody.

She wouldn't give me any names because if "they" knew it would make things worse. I needed to win her trust and I told her quietly that I had ways of dealing with these situations that wouldn't make them worse, but that I needed the girls' names so that I could speak to them, and that I especially needed the name of the older girl of whom she was so frightened. Eventu- ally she gave it to me: "Carol Harris."

Inside me a little voice said, "Damn!" I had used the No Blame

Approach a few times, but usually with people that I had something positive to work on. Now I had to try it with a girl who had hated me for nearly four years, a girl who hated me because I had suggested that she was a bully! Could it work? I had to try but I wished that I hadn't promised Angela quite so confidently that things would be all right.

I met Carol in the corridor.

"Carol."

"Yeah." She looked at me with that "what have I done now?" look.

"Could you come into my office for a few minutes."

She followed me, her body language giving away her unwillingness. When we reached my office, I beckoned her to sit on one of the comfy chairs usually reserved for visitors. I sat on the chair beside her.

"Thank you for coming, Carol." I smiled.

She looked suspicious. Why was I being nice to her?

"I wanted to speak to you, Carol, because I'm really worried about Angela White. She's feeling really bad because of this business with Jane, and now she's worried because she's heard that you and your friends are going to get involved. She's frightened because she has heard that you're going to "get" her after school. I've told her that I'm sure this isn't true, but she doesn't believe me. Have you heard anything about it?"

The meeting explored various possibilities and solutions were discussed. The conversation ended with "Good girl." At this, Carol looked really surprised. I was calling her a good girl! But she looked pleased...

"In the meantime I'll speak to Jane and check what has been said. If Angela has said anything, I'll get her to apologise. But it's best that I handle it. OK?"

"OK."

"Thanks, Carol. I'll get back to you later to see how things are going." Carol left my office with no feelings of resentment; after all, she had nothing to feel resentful about. I had merely outlined the situation to her, but no blame had been apportioned."

The account then relates how this type of interaction can change relationships.

The next day when I saw Carol I asked,
     "How are things going?"
     "Fine, I apologised to Angela and it all seems OK now."
     "Good girl."
She smiled. Twice in as many days I had told her she was a good girl. From that day to the day that she left, as we passed each other in the corridor, we would smile at each other, or sometimes Carol would say, "Hi, Miss." I couldn't believe the transformation. Other staff noticed it too.

As I reflect on this, and think about Carol, I realise that my first dealings with her only served to reinforce her low self-esteem. She was one of twins, and her sister was totally different, diligent and successful in her work, quiet, and never in trouble, whereas during her four years with us Carol had often been in trouble, and each time the difference between her and her sister must have been reinforced in her mind. As for me, when I had first dealt with Carol I had given her no opportunity to understand the hurt her behaviour had caused, nor to put things right herself. I had responded in anger, labelled her a "bully", and then used my authority to "bully" her into submission. The result of this was an increased resentment on her part, so much so that further dealings with her about her misbehaviour had been perceived as me "having it in for her" once more. However the last time I had "dealt" with her she had been able to take some responsibility for her actions, change her behaviour and restore her self-respect. Instead of a negative relationship with me, a positive one had emerged, and through this Carol became more able to feel more positive about herself. If only I had been able to use the No Blame Approach on that first occasion, what a different Carol we might have seen during the next four years..."

Crying for Help

We do not claim that we have presented watertight research and evaluation in previous writing or in this book. However, when you hear comments that the No Blame Approach has not been rigorously, independently evaluated, compare our evidence with other approaches. You will find that there are only a small number of interventions available to deal with incidents of bullying:

1 We support Peer Mediation, though this has not been well researched in bullying.

2 We have reservations about Peer Counselling because we know that counselling is a rigorous discipline. The limited training offered to the pupil counsellors might expose them to tasks and responsibilities beyond the capabilities of a young person.

3 We totally reject punitive responses such as bully courts and wait with anticipation for any independent research evidence which supports the effectiveness of detentions, suspensions or exclusions to stop bullying and protect victims.

We offer this book as a valid statement that non-punitive, problem-solving approaches which seek to empower young people through encouraging empathic and altruistic responses offer a safer and more effective response that is no more time-consuming than the traditional punitive intervention.

We do not offer a magic wand. The No Blame Approach will not work in every situation but if it doesn't work the first time try it again. If it still doesn't work, try changing the group.

Changes in society are initiated in many ways and academic research findings do play an important part in this process. Good practice, training and influence are also effective methods and researchers should not dismiss popular movements as invalid or unreliable. The voices of participants are part of research methodology and should not be ignored.

Andrew's Postscript   July 1997

We started this book with a story from 1991; we can finish the story in 1997.

"A few years after the events described earlier I received a message to phone Andrew's father. I was a surprised, and a little puzzled, as there had been no contact since Andrew had celebrated his 'A'- level success at our presentation evening. When I returned the call I was delighted to hear that Andrew had successfully completed a degree course. Andrew's father wanted to say thank you for the intervention when Andrew was being bullied and to let me know how successful he had been from then on."

Head of Sixth Form

For at least one pupil, the No Blame Approach made a difference for life.

Bibliography

ATTWOOD, M. (1990) Cat's Eye. London, Virago Press.

BESAG, V.E. (1989) Bullies and Victims in Schools. Milton Keynes, O.U.P.

BESAG, V. E. (1992) We Don't Have Bullies Here. 57, Manor House Road, Newcastle Upon Tyne.

BRAITHWAITE, J. (1989) Crime, Shame and Reintegration. Cambridge, Cambridge Univ. Press.

DfE. (1994) Bullying, Don't suffer in silence. London, H.M.S.O.

DAVIES, J.G.V. & MALIPHANT, R. (1974) Refractory Behaviour in School and Avoidance Learning. Journal of Child Psychology and Psychiatry Vol. 15 p 23 - 31

ELLIOTT, M. (ed) (1991) Bullying: a practical guide to coping for schools. Longman, in association with Kidscape.

FOSTER, P. ARORA, T. & THOMPSON, D. (1990) An example of one school's approach to the task of developing a whole school policy. Pastoral Care in Education. September 1990.

GORDON,T. (1974) Teacher Effectiveness Training. New York, Wyden.

JONES, E. (1991) Practical considerations in dealing with bullying in secondary schools, in Bullying: a practical guide to coping for schools. Longman in association with Kidscape, edited by Michelle Elliott.

MAINES, B. & ROBINSON, G. (1990) You can...You know you can. Bristol, Lucky Duck Publishing.

MAINES, B. & ROBINSON, G. (1991) Teacher Talk. Bristol, Lucky Duck Publishing.

MAINES, B. & ROBINSON, G. (1991b) Stamp out Bullying. Bristol, Lucky Duck Publishing.

MAINES, B. & ROBINSON, G. (1991) Punishment, The Milder the Better. Bristol, Lucky Duck Publishing.

MAINES, B. & ROBINSON, G. (1992) The No Blame Approach. (video and training booklet) Bristol, Lucky Duck Publishing.

MAINES, B. & ROBINSON, G. (1994a) The No Blame Approach to Bullying. A Paper presented to the British Association for the Advancement of Science.

MAINES,B. & ROBINSON, G. (1994b) If it makes my life Easier... to write a Policy on Bullying. Bristol, Lucky Duck Publishing.

MAINES, B. & ROBINSON, G. (1995) Parent Leaflet on Bullying. Bristol, Lucky Duck Publishing.

MUNRO, S. (1997) Overcome Bullying for Parents. London, Piccadilly Press.

OLWEUS, D. (1978) Aggression in the Schools: Bullies and Whipping-boys. London, Wiley; Halsted Press.

OLWEUS, D. (1987) Bully/Victim Problems among School Children in Scandinavia, in Myklebust J. & Ommundsen R. (eds) Psykologprofessionen mot år 2000. Oslo Universitetsførlaget.

PEARCE, J. (1991) What can be done about the bully? in Bullying: a practical guide to coping for schools. Longman, in association with Kidscape, edited by Michelle Elliott.

PIKAS, A. (1975) Treatment of Mobbing in School: Principles for and the results of the work of an anti mobbing group. Scandinavian Journal of Education Research.

PIKAS, A. (1989) The Common Concern Method for the Treatment of Mobbing: in Roland, E. & Munthe, E. Bullying: An International Perspective. London, David Fulton.

RIGBY, K. (1996) Bullying in Schools and what to do about it. London, Jessica Kingsley.

ROBINSON,G., SLEIGH,J. AND MAINES,B. (1995) No Bullying Starts Today, Bristol, Lucky Duck Publishing.

ROLAND, E. and MUNTHE, E. (eds) (1989) Bullying, An International Perspective. London, David Fulton.

SCRE (1991) - Scottish Council for Research in Education. Action Against Bullying.

SCRE (1993) - Scottish Council for Research in Education. Supporting Schools against Bullying.

SHARP, S. & SMITH, P.K. (eds) (1994) Tackling Bullying in your school: A Practical Handbook for Teachers. London, Routledge.

SMITH, P.K. & SHARP, S. (eds) (1994) School Bullying, Insights and Perspectives. London, Routledge.

STEPHENSON, P. and SMITH, D. (1989) Bullying in the junior school: in Tattum, D. and Lane, D. (eds), Bullying in Schools.

STRAW, J. (1995) Burdened by Memories of Bullying. Daily Mirror, January 18th.

United Nations (1989) The Convention on the Rights of the Child. Adopted by the General Assembly of the United Nations on 20th November 1989.

YATES, C. & SMITH, P. (1989) Bullying in two English Comprehensive Schools: in Roland, E. & Munthe, E. (eds) Bullying, An International Perspective. London, David Fulton.

YOSHIO, M. (1985) Bullies in the Classroom. Japan Quarterly. Vol. 32, p. 407-411.

YOUNG, S. (1998) The Support Group Approach to Bullying in Schools. Educational Psychology in Practice, Vol. 14. No. 1, P32-39.

Don't forget to visit our website for all our latest publications, news and reviews.

www.luckyduck.co.uk

New publications every year on our specialist topics:

- ▶ **Emotional Literacy**
- ▶ **Self-esteem**
- ▶ **Bullying**
- ▶ **Positive Behaviour Management**
- ▶ **Circle Time**
- ▶ **Anger Management**
- ▶ **Asperger's Syndrome**
- ▶ **Eating Disorders**

3 Thorndale Mews, Clifton, Bristol, BS8 2HX | Tel: +44 (0) 117 973 2881 Fax: +44 (0) 117 973 1707